PRAISE FOR GARY COLLINS

Cabot Island

"Collins' focus on an ordinary event taking place under extraordinary circumstances sheds a tender, respectful light on how strength of character can be forged at the anguished intersection of isolation and bereavement."
DOWNHOME

"The story is intriguing . . ."
THE CHRONICLE HERALD

The Last Farewell

"The writing here is at its best when the danger and beauty of the sea is subtly described." — ATLANTIC BOOKS TODAY

"*The Last Farewell* tells a true story, but Collins' vivid description and well-realized characters make it read like a novel." — THE CHRONICLE HERALD

"Read *The Last Farewell* not only because it is a moving historical tale of needless tragedy but also because it's a book enriched with abundant details of Newfoundland life not so widespread anymore."— THE PILOT

"[*The Last Farewell:*] *The Loss of the Collett* is informative and intriguing, and not merely for experienced sailors or Newfoundlanders." — THE NORTHERN MARINER

MORE PRAISE FOR GARY COLLINS

Soulis Joe's Lost Mine

"There is a magic in the interior of this island that few will write about or speak of to others—an endless fascination with the land. Gary Collins is entranced in the same way that the allure of rock, tree, and bog seized the indomitable Allan Keats, and before him, his ancestor, the Mi'kmaq Soulis Joe. This book gives voice not only to these men but to the great and wonderful wilderness of Newfoundland. Read it and be prepared for the wonder and love of the wild places. It will grab and hold on to you, too." — J.A. RICKETTS, AUTHOR OF *THE BADGER CONFESSION*

"*Soulis Joe's Lost Mine* is a number of stories in one: it's a great mystery-adventure; it's a fascinating look at prospecting for precious metals; and it's a heart-warming story about the importance of family pride."
THE CHRONICLE HERALD

"This tale also serves to cement Collins' status as one of the region's better storytellers; he has a journalist's eye for detail, his writing is crisp and lean and the narrative arc runs smooth and seamless and is well-peppered with shakes of home-spun humour." — ATLANTIC BOOKS TODAY

MORE PRAISE FOR GARY COLLINS

What Colour is the Ocean?

"Delightful rhyming story."
RESOURCE LINKS

"Scott Keating's illustrations are an asset to the book. The double page illustrations revealing the colour of the ocean are particularly successful in conveying the moods of the ocean and the land." — CM: CANADIAN REVIEW OF MATERIALS

"This tale, set by the sea in Newfoundland, is told in a simple repetitive refrain that will capture the imagination of young readers. . . . Illustrations by Scott Keating, award-winning artist and illustrator, capture the beauty of Newfoundland and the many seasons and moods of the ocean." — ATLANTIC BOOKS TODAY

Where Eagles Lie Fallen

"Some truly breathtaking stories of tragedy . . ."
THE NORTHEAST AVALON TIMES

"A gripping story,
which cuts to the true heart of tragedy."
DOWNHOME

Other books by Gary Collins

Mattie Mitchell

NEWFOUNDLAND'S GREATEST FRONTIERSMAN

Mattie Mitchell

NEWFOUNDLAND'S GREATEST FRONTIERSMAN

GARY COLLINS

FLANKER PRESS LIMITED
ST. JOHN'S
2011

Library and Archives Canada Cataloguing in Publication

Collins, Gary, 1949-
Mattie Mitchell : Newfoundland's greatest
frontiersman / Gary Collins.

Includes bibliographical references.
Also issued in electronic format.
ISBN 978-1-926881-01-0

1. Mitchell, Mattie, 1850-1921. 2. Micmac Indians--Newfoundland
and Labrador--Biography. 3. Prospectors--Newfoundland and
Labrador--Biography. 4. Loggers--Newfoundland and Labrador--
Biography. 5. Fishing guides--Newfoundland and Labrador--Biography.
6. Hunting guides--Newfoundland and Labrador--Biography. 7. Frontier
and pioneer life--Newfoundland and Labrador. I. Title.

FC2173.1.M58C64 2011   971.8004'973430092   C2011-907125-8

PRINTED IN CANADA

Cover Photo: Mattie Mitchell with salmon, taken in Lomond River, circa 1918.
Photo by D.K. Boyd, donated by Colin Boyd.

Cover Design: Peter Hanes   Illustration and cover art by Clint Collins

FLANKER PRESS LTD.
PO BOX 2522, STATION C
ST. JOHN'S, NL
CANADA

TELEPHONE: (709) 739-4477   FAX: (709) 739-4420   TOLL-FREE: 1-866-739-4420
WWW.FLANKERPRESS.COM

16 15 14 13 12   3 4 5 6 7 8 9 10

We acknowledge the financial support of the Government of Canada through the Book Publishing Industry Development Program (BPIDP) for our publishing activities; the Canada Council for the Arts which last year invested $24.3 million in writing and publishing throughout Canada; the Government of Newfoundland and Labrador, Department of Tourism, Culture and Recreation

I respectfully dedicate this book to Marie Marion Sparkes née Mitchell, whom, sadly, I never met. She passed from this earth before I started to write about her grandfather, Mattie Mitchell.

And grasps me now a long-unwonted yearning
For that serene and solemn Spirit-Land:
My song, to faint Aeolian murmurs turning,
Sways like a harp-string by the breezes fanned.
I thrill and tremble; tear on tear is burning,
And the stern heart is tenderly unmanned.
What I possess, I see far distant lying,
And what I lost, grows real and undying.

Goethe's *Faust*

PREFACE

THE TIME I SPENT WRITING ABOUT the incredible life of Mattie Mitchell the frontiersman has been a joyous one. The wilds of Newfoundland have always been a sacred, mysterious place for me. As Mattie's pages lengthened, so did my respect for the man. When the manuscript was nearing completion, I was hired along with my partner, Allan Keats, to spend the summer prospecting in the wilderness of Newfoundland. One of the areas we worked was the Great Northern Peninsula. I could not believe my good fortune! I would be paid to traverse the same country where Mattie Mitchell had spent the most exciting part of his life.

For thirty days Al and I drove, canoed, and walked most of the area between Gunners Cove in the north to Daniel's Harbour in the south. And as we walked the land, with maps, compass, and GPS in hand, my respect for Mattie Mitchell grew daily. This area of our province truly is great! There is no other place like it. Away from the stunted, twisted tuckamore trees that line the coastal gulf highway there lies a hidden world.

Among the distant mountains of grandeur there are hanging green valleys of incredible beauty. Untouched forests of fragrant balsam firs, gun-barrel-straight drokes of black spruce, and stately, castor-scented white spruce grow in profusion. Twisting along the mountain valleys, the clearest of river waters course along limestone beds and sometimes mysteriously disappear without a trace. From the heights one can see endless vistas of the distant ocean sheltering white-clad villages. Verdant green hills and deep valley winds fill your senses.

This is an area of our province about which few south of that peninsula know. It is more than worth it to take a day's journey off the beaten path. It is a hunter's paradise, a photographer's delight, and it will test the mettle of the most ardent hiker. And always, the great mountains will witness your journey. The place truly amazed me and will forever stay with me.

Somewhere, in one of the hidden valleys we walked through, I found the true spirit of Mattie Mitchell. It was more than the mere admiration for a man who could travel across this great land without any of the modern navigational aids Al and I carried. That fact in itself astounded me.

No, it was the realization of the man's true being: he had been one with such a vast wilderness. This knowledge finally connected me spiritually to a great man I had never met, but with whom I have gladly walked.

SEPTEMBER, 2011
HARE BAY, NL

CHAPTER 1

EVER SINCE SHE WAS OLD ENOUGH to hear the adults in her family tell their stories, Marie Marion Mitchell was an avid listener and something more. As she grew, Marie learned that she was blessed with a near-photographic memory.

She was born in the Newfoundland west coast city of Corner Brook on May 20, 1936. She was baptized in the Roman Catholic faith in that same city on May 24 of the same year at the Holy Redeemer Cathedral Parish.

Her childhood years were a time without television. Her family owned a dry-cell battery-operated radio. It was the only mechanical source of entertainment in their home. Between the bouts of static emerging from the radio—turned on only at night—came the crackly voice of a newsman. It was not entertaining to a child. Marie's favourite source of amusement and entertainment came from the stories she heard in her mother's kitchen.

She remembered cold winters evenings especially. The kitchen door would open without anyone knocking, and stepping through the doorway with a brief kick of their feet to dislodge the snow caked to their boots, their visitors would enter. Great drafts of cold winter air came with them, meeting the warmth of the kitchen to produce misty wreaths above the hats that covered their heads.

It was almost always men of the Mi'kmaq race who came. They were hunters who knew the ways of the wilds, and they came to tell their stories. They also knew their own oral history. Their favourite stories to tell were of the man who was a legend in their world, Mattie Mitchell. And while they spun their yarns, Marie listened with all of her attention. She never tired of hearing about her famous grandfather.

The rugged men with bristly beards smoked short-stemmed pipes or thin cigarettes they rolled themselves. As they talked, the room warmed and they removed their coats, but never their boots. Smoke leaving their mouths was drawn by the heat of the wood range and, rising blue above the hot stove, escaped through the seam between the black funnel and the silver flange nailed to the white ceiling.

This was where the young Marie first heard about Mattie Mitchell. Without knowing it, she was holding in her head the storied history of a man who was legend among his people. And from her memory she would record in her personal journals the incredible lore she had heard about the grandfather she always wished she had known.

* * * * *

MATTIE, IT SEEMED, HAD AN affinity toward rivers. Maybe it was because the man was intelligent enough to realize that river valleys almost always provided easy access into the wilderness. All river valleys are conduits for game, whose ceaseless wanderings established trails for the knowing traveller. Or maybe it was simply Mattie's love for the romance of a swift river and burbling stream that spawned some of the stories Marie cherished.

He found ruby red and emerald green garnets and jaspers on Flat Bay Brook and the Humber River. He knew where to find a coal seam on the Humber. He found a salt deposit on Crabb's Brook.

And on one of the rivers that flow into the Bay St. George, he found gold. For many years the tale of Mattie Mitchell's gold was figured to be just a tall tale. Mattie was finding his way along the shoreline of a river one day in late autumn. The day was late. The sun was settling down among the trees, its lowering light blazing through the trees and glinting on the rushing water as it sank. He carried upon his broad shoulders a pack heavily laden with animal skins. In one hand he carried his heavy Martin Henry rifle. In his other hand was a long-handled, broad-faced axe.

He was returning to the coast after a month-long trapping venture. He was taking his furs to the only furrier on the coast he trusted to give him a fair price.

Mattie rarely saw any money from his work. His furs—always in prime condition and well cured—he exchanged for provisions for his family. His own needs were simple: tea and salt and, if he was lucky, sugar, a small bag of gunpowder, and a handful of bullets would do him just fine. Mattie traded the bulk of his furs for his family's needs before he set off once again into the wilderness.

His way had been long. The autumn had been warm and unusually dry. River bottoms showed. Some of the brooks and streams had slowed to a trickle. Yellowing birches and golden aspens shed shrivelled leaves that rustled noisily down, crisp and weathered. The broad lower branches of the white spruce trees discarded their sun-burnt reddish brown tips as he brushed past them. The pungent, musky smell that comes with late autumn rains, which every true hunter loves, was missing. It was a time without rain. Mattie had journeyed along this waterway many times, but he had never seen the water level so low.

He was picking his way over a rocky riverbank when the sunlight filtering through the trees reflected off a shiny white surface just ahead of him. When he reached the rock formation he saw a narrow vein running down through the reddish outcrop. Mattie knew the white, crystalline rock in the vein was quartz. He had learned about quartz veins, in particular that they appeared in rust-coloured rocks, from his time guiding geologists. They always paid attention to such places and hammered away at the rocks with the backs of their axes, sometimes studying the pieces for hours. And as they talked, Mattie listened and never forgot.

The low water level had revealed the vein. Mattie lowered his load to the ground and approached the white vein, axe in hand. Settling onto his haunches, he studied the rock. The quartz vein was no more than five inches wide, but it ran from the bank and disappeared under the river water. Mattie scanned the other side of the river but could see no sign that the rock formation had reached across. Looking again at the cliff and noticing the steep angle at which it entered the water, he calculated that it went deep underground at the river's centre.

A brownish cliff several feet wide bordered the quartz on either side. With the back of his axe, Mattie broke a large piece of the white rock loose. The rock was very heavy. He turned it over in his hand and immediately saw the yellow sheen of gold flakes!

Brown stains ran throughout the fractures in the rock. In places the quartz appeared grey. It also smelled bad. Stinky quartz, the geologists had called it. Pyrite cubes glittered everywhere, but the "fool's gold" did not trick Mattie. The pyrite appeared to have been placed into the rock, and its colour changed when he turned it against the dying sun. But the gold seemed to be spattered into the rock, and no matter how he shifted it around, it never lost its deep lustre. He broke several more pieces away and was rewarded again with the buttery colour.

Mattie was neither excited or surprised at his discovery. It was just something his quick eye had found. His remarkable power of recall had done the rest to conjure up the memories of his time with Alexander Murray and James Howley.

Walking back to where he had laid down his pack, with several pieces of the rock cradled in his hands, he thought for a minute where he would put the samples. The day was late and he was hungry. He would not make the coast before dark. He decided to spend the night here on the wooded, mossy bank of the river.

Mattie soon had a small campfire going below the high riverbank. He filled his quart-sized kettle, which was long blackened and dented, with water from the river. Hooking the kettle from a green alder by its wire handle and placing it over the crackling fire, he climbed up over the bank and prepared to build a shelter for the night.

Steam rising from the fire caught his eye. At first he thought the water had boiled over. As he neared the fire, he heard the hiss of water falling on hot coals. His kettle was leaking! He pulled it away from the fire and dumped the few drops left onto the ground. Holding the kettle against the sky, he saw two small holes in its bottom. Resigning himself to a dry meal, he was about to throw the kettle away when he remembered his gold. The kettle was still strong and would make an excellent container in which to carry the rocks.

The next morning broke cold and misty, but the rising sun soon burned through the "pride of the morning," and when Mattie loaded the heavy pack on his shoulders, the day was warm. Mattie picked up the heavy kettle and considered how he would carry it. It would surely make a noise if he carried it in either hand along with his gun and axe. He fully intended to have a goose or a couple of ducks before he reached the end of this day's travel, so the kettle would have to remain behind.

He scraped a hole in the coarse gravel under the riverbank and placed the kettle inside. Then he filled in the shallow hole with the gravel and placed several heavy rocks on top of it. He shouldered his pack again and without once looking back he walked away down the bright river valley. The years went by and Mattie never returned for his "kettle of gold." He told the story of his gold find many times. Everyone listened to him. Some believed him. But without the "golden" proof, many did not. The river rose and fell with the seasons. Some years its waters peaked and some seasons they did not. Mattie's golden kettle was forgotten.

Until one late summer day in 1943.

* * * * *

THE LUSH, GREEN FARMLANDS ON THE coastal plain around the largely French-speaking town of Stephenville on Newfoundland's southwest coast had been converted to one of the world's biggest runways. War had come lording over the lands of the earth. Since 1939, the free peoples of Europe had been fighting against a tyranny unequalled in history. The isles of Britain, the plains of southern Europe, and the deserts of North Africa were fierce battlegrounds. On December 7, 1941, the richest nation on earth declared war against the far-off nation of Japan. And now the dogs of war scoured the globe, snarling and fighting as they went.

Stephenville had become an American base of more than 8,000 acres. The airstrips created there on the edge of the western sea were 150 feet wide and stretched 6,000 feet toward the distant mountains. During the peak war years from 1943-1945, more than 30,000 American troops per year passed through the base at Harmon Field.

Day and night the planes came in from the western gulf which separated the island nation of Newfoundland from the land mass of Canada. And just as regularly they flew away again, heading for distant battles that went on and on. And when it was over, all of the dead names could fill pages of books that would never be written. The Greek philosopher Plato said it best: Only the dead have seen the last of war.

Mattie Mitchell's bones had long since blended into the earth he so dearly loved when a young American airman came walking up the river valley. He was accompanied by another man who was little more than a teenager. The American's nickname was "Stringer." He was the leader of his squadron. When he came roaring in from the Atlantic for the airstrip at Stephenville, he always had a group of fighter planes in his "string."

Stringer had met and fallen in love with a local dark-haired girl. The young airman was an avid fly fisherman who until now had never tried his hand at fishing for Atlantic salmon. Stringer learned that his fiancé's younger brother knew all about fishing for salmon. The brother and sister were of Mi'kmaq descent. And so it was that the two men made their way up the river where Mattie Mitchell had found gold so many decades ago. They headed toward a deep pool where the boy assured the airman the salmon always rested.

For two hours the American fished the deep, dark water of the pool without any success, although the salmon frequently jumped all around him. He had changed his fly hooks several times, but it was all in vain. He just couldn't get the hang of catching an Atlantic salmon. Walking a little farther upstream and pulling his hat from his head, he removed another fly hook from the felt band that ran around the quiff. He was tying the fly to the fine leader when he saw it.

He bent his head down and placed the end of the barrel knot between his teeth. Turning his head sideways, he bit down and severed the line. A sparkle of yellow shone up through the shallow water at his feet. At first Stringer thought it was the sunlight on the water surface. More curious than anything, he bent down to investigate. With his rod held in the crook of his left arm, he reached into the water with his right hand.

Stringer was surprised to feel metal. He pulled, and it came free from the gravelly bottom. There came a rattle of sound muffled by the water. What he pulled from the river bottom appeared to be a small metal can with only the upper edge remaining. Only rusted shards remained of the container's sides and nothing of the bottom part. Looking down into the water, the yellow sparkle still remained. Stringer discarded the rusted can and reached into the water again. When he brought his hand out of the water, it was filled with rocks that glittered with gold flakes. When Stringer's shouts brought his guide to his side, the young Mi'kmaq said with excitement, "You have found Mattie's kettle o' gold!"

For days after, the story of the golden rocks was on everyone's lips. It even made the local media. Many people still remembered the tale of Mattie's kettle of gold. Several hurried expeditions travelled up the river to find more of the precious metal, but none was found.

* * * * *

ANOTHER STORY INVOLVING MATTIE and a river is that of the "duckish water." It shows the wit and humour of the man.

For several days Mattie had been walking upstream from the coast, tending his autumn traps. Early each morning, whenever he approached one deep, muddy cove in particular, away from the main current—formed by one of the river's many back eddies— he would disturb a small flock of ducks. At his approach, the ducks always battered away upriver and squawked in protest.

One day Mattie was asked to take two English sportsmen hunting. The two hunters had been told that Mattie knew all there was to know about fish and birds. Mattie had overheard the conversation and as usual made no comment. The river valley where he always saw the ducks was easy going for the most part. It also happened to fall in the same general direction he wanted to take the two hunters. On the first morning out with the two Englishmen, Mattie stopped 200 feet or so before the spot where he expected to see the ducks. He approached the cool river water and bent down to take a drink. Sitting back with his mouth full, he rinsed the water back and forth several times before swallowing. Slowly and deliberately, he cupped his hand into the stream again and sucked the water through his lips, giving his two companions the impression that he was deep in thought over something. Apparently satisfied, he spat the water out of his mouth and announced to no one in particular that the water "taste duckish, maybe."

One of the sportsmen stood over him asked, "Whatever do you mean, my good fellow?"

"The water taste like duck. Black ones, maybe. Dey not far upriver. Round next ben', maybe," Mattie said with a straight face.

The two men turned away from Mattie and mumbled something about crazy natives. When they rounded the next bend in the river, sure enough, up flew the small flock of ducks, much to the delight of a smiling Mattie and the chagrin of the English hunters. As the ducks flew away without one shot fired at them, Mattie heard one of the men exclaim, "By jove! Blacks, too!"

* * * * *

THE TALES OF MATTIE MITCHELL'S exploits—all of them adventurous—told by the men who visited the house of John

Mitchell, Marie's father, seemed endless. And always the pretty, black-haired girl with the dark eyes listened and remembered.

* * * * *

MATTIE WENT ON ONE OF THE LAST of his adventures in 1910. He wasn't searching for natural treasures but for something quite different: pirate treasure.

From the sixteenth century the eastern shores of the Americas were a mecca for pirates. The "new" world offered fresh opportunities for those who dared to take their fortune rather than earn it. Today their names roll off the tongue of every schoolboy. They are all infamous. Edward Teach, or Blackbeard, as the world knew him, plundered his nefarious way all along the American coast of colonies. Black Bart and Captain Kidd were men whose very names brought dread to every honest captain. Henry Morgan was a Welshman who razed the city of Panama and terrorized the West Indies. He held command of an entire ocean for a time. They were all sea thieves from the past. But there was one other pirate whose daring outshone them all—Peter Easton.

From his base in Newfoundland, Easton sailed as far west as the Barbary Coast of northwest Africa. He commanded a crew of thousands in as many as forty ships. Many of his crewmen were volunteers, but it is believed that he had taken the vast majority aboard his ships by force. He was the scourge of John Guy, who had established the first English colony in Newfoundland. By 1610, Easton was considered the most powerful pirate in the western hemisphere.

Easton would steal a shipload of salted-down fish headed from Newfoundland to England just as soon as he would take a ship laden with rum and spices from the Indies. Stolen doubloons and pieces of eight from Spain, and beaver pelts from English merchants all meant the same to Peter Easton—money. Several countries on either side of the Atlantic followed and hounded the much-feared corsair, but he was never captured.

It was said that Easton hid some of his ill-gotten wealth in several places around the Newfoundland coast. One such place was reported to be the small Shell Bird Island, just upstream from the wide mouth of the Humber River. Mattie Mitchell had heard all of these white man stories. He had passed Shell Bird Island many times over the course of his lifetime. Once, he stopped there and explored the place, but found nothing.

Another place Easton had supposedly hidden treasure was on another island, St. John Island, on the Newfoundland side of the Strait of Belle Isle. Local legend tells of a pirate ship that ran aground near the island while seeking shelter from a fierce storm that tore up the strait. Fearing their ship would founder, the pirates removed chests of gold coins and precious jewels from the tossing vessel and hid them on the island, well above the high-water mark. The storm abated without causing any significant damage to their ship, and the pirates hurried to catch the high tide and sailed away from the land. They had scratched an arrow into a boulder to mark the location of the treasure, for which they would return. The arrow and the boulder were visible only at very low tide. According to the legend, the pirates were besieged by another, more violent storm. The ship and all hands were lost.

Mattie Mitchell knew St. John Island very well. It was a part of his hunting grounds. He had erected a small shelter there. He had also been there many times at the request of people hoping to recover the pirate treasure. Those who paid the small fee for his services hoped the old woodsman's eyes would reveal what so many others had failed to see. But Mattie could find no trace of the treasure. Eventually, he refused to take any more fortune seekers there again. Like everyone else, he figured the pirates and their gold were a myth.

Then, one cold winter's day near the end of 1910, while travelling along his trapline far inland from his home in Bonne Bay, he met an old man who had a map to the pirate gold.

Mattie was accompanied by one of his wife's relatives. The young boy from the Webb family was learning the ways of the wild from the best of hunters and trappers. The short winter day was late and the sun had gone. Night was near, and there was no warmth upon the land. Suddenly, across their trail, an old man staggered and abruptly fell. Mattie and his young companion half dragged, half carried the emaciated man to their camp, which fortunately was nearby.

Mattie fed the man with hot caribou broth and, as he grew stronger, caribou meat. He laid the old man in his own warm bunk and covered him, where he slept on his back without stirring for twelve hours. The man's hair was wild and snow white. He was balding in front. His exposed brown scalp furrowed a path through a patch of unruly long hair that fell to his narrow shoulders, so that the man's face appeared to be staring out of a tangled bush. He looked to be very old, but the energy behind his bright blue eyes contradicted his age.

For several days Mattie and the young boy nursed their patient back to health. In all that time they never once asked him how he had come to be in these northern woods. The man had tremendous resilience; he soon recovered and appeared to be strong enough to travel. When Mattie invited him to accompany them to the coast, he very politely declined. The stranger thanked his two rescuers, but he said he would be all right now and prepared to leave.

Standing in the dim light of the small cabin, the old man produced a faded map. He explained to Mattie that if he followed the map precisely he would find enough gold to provide not only for him, but his entire family for the rest of their lives. The map revealed the location of the pirate treasure of St. John Island. The man handed Mattie the map, shook hands with him and Webb, and wished them a very Merry Christmas before walking out the door and disappearing down the snowy trail.

The very next year, Mattie and a friend made their way up the Northern Peninsula to Eddies Cove. Tucked safely inside his pack in a waterproof satchel was the treasure map given to him by the old man of the hills. Upon reaching the small village of Eddies Cove late in the evening, Mattie finally persuaded Joe Offrey to take him and his companion across to St. John Island. They had enough supplies for an extended stay. This time Mattie—armed with the old man's map—figured he would find the fabled pirate treasure.

Using the old man's yellowed map, Mattie found, at low tide, a small arrow etched into a boulder. He found other marks, but none of them were easy to find. It took a keen and very observant eye to follow the aged map.

But it was not to be. The old woodsman suffered a stroke and, with the help of his friend, returned home without ever finding the treasure. He would never return to St. John Island again. The island with the pirate treasure is still a legend.

* * * * *

FOR MARIE MITCHELL, THE WINTER NIGHTS when the men talked their trail talk were openings into the world of her grandfather, one she would never see with her own eyes. But inside her head the tales would forever remain as vivid as the nights when she had first heard them.

Marie remembered her first movies about cowboys and Indians. The Indians were always the bad guys and never won any of the battles. Around her in the theatre all of her friends had shouted "Shoot the redskins!" All she could do was stay quiet and wonder why.

Remembering the days of her childhood, Marie still felt the sting of prejudice. The taunts of "Marie is nothing but an Injun" coming from her peers was anything but funny to her. But through it all she remained steadfast to her heritage. Nothing would sway her from the pride she felt of who she was. And she was proudest of all that her grandfather was the one and only Mattie Mitchell.

In 1946, Marie was ten years old and in the fifth grade. One day, as she sat in her classroom in Corner Brook, she heard the teacher speak the name of Mattie Mitchell. She timidly raised her hand and in a quiet, shaky voice said, "That's my grandfather, Miss."

Her teacher hushed the other children, who were laughing at Marie. Marie finally convinced the teacher that her statement was true. The other kids stared at her in awe: she had a connection to a figure in their Newfoundland history school book!

Bursting with pride, Marie raced home and informed her parents of the sentence in her Newfoundland geography book, the one that said her grandfather had discovered the mine in Buchans. Her parents, who of course knew about Mattie's discovery, were thrilled to learn that Mattie Mitchell's name was living on in Marie's generation.

From that day forward, Marie started a lifelong quest to record all known information about her legendary grandfather. Her dedication to the task ended only with her death.

CHAPTER 2

THE HIGH GREY MOUNTAINS WITH their wondrous mystery were silent. Their vast, white, flat-topped plateaus draped behind dark evening clouds. It was late March, but the hills and valleys on Newfoundland's west coast were still choked with heavy winter snow. A mist had drizzled from the low-hanging clouds all day. It was a sly, sneaky moisture that seeped through a man's clothing and soaked the skin almost without his knowing. Now with night shadows climbing up through the deep-wooded valleys below, the rain got colder.

Mattie Mitchell was soaked to the bone. His coarse, black woollen clothes, most of it showing sparse herring-bone patches of his own careful stitching, were plastered to his tawny skin. Despite the cold rain, Mattie was sweating. The mild temperature along with the rain made the snow soft underfoot, and although the trail he followed was well packed, he sank through in places. The trail wound its twisted way through a mature virgin forest. At intervals, open spaces between the trees allowed Mattie a view of the distant ridges. They showed blue against the slate sky. Tiny tendrils of steam emanated from beneath his worn coat collar and, like the last rising images of heat from a dying campfire, vanished into the air.

The worn thin straps from a dirty grey canvas pack bit into his tired shoulders. Inside the pack were the pelts of three fox—two with thick red hides and one with a shiny black coat. One fawn-tinted lynx and three brunette beaver skins, the lush hide of one partly cured "marten cat," several pounds of cured caribou meat, and a few meagre personal belongings filled his pack to its laced mouth. Lashed securely to the outside of the pack was a large unskinned beaver with its broad tail dangling below.

More than two hours' walk behind, Mattie had pulled the furred rodent from its watery grave beneath the ice of a small pond, reset the steel trap, and walked on. Running under the heavy pack, angled upward and crossing his forehead ran a two-inch-wide leather thump line. It was a simple and practical native design that relieved much of the weight from the lower back and transferred it to the neck and head.

Now, standing on the edge of a high, snow-covered alpine meadow, he paused. He had not stopped for a rest since he had shrugged the dead beaver into place onto his broad shoulders miles back. Weary and nearing the place where he would find rest, Mattie scanned the deep, white valley below him. He couldn't see the river that ran the length of the winter valley, but he knew it was there, even without hearing the sound of its waters rising and falling on the evening breeze. What he could see of the distant elevation through the misty rain showed a dark blue. It was another sure sign of a mild spell. Maybe it was time to leave for the coast, he thought.

The man who stood looking down into the wet, misty valley was tall. He was several inches taller than six feet. His small, far-seeing eyes were dark, like the deep colour of a perfectly cured pine marten hide. His face was long and angular, and his full head of thick black hair fell matted below his ears. His jaws and well-defined cheekbones were clean of facial hair, though he seldom shaved. His mouth was full, below a straight, full nose that belied his ancestry. Mattie Mitchell was a handsome man. He looked as if some hidden gene had been lodged in his veins, producing in his features, for all to see, the link of his mysterious lineage.

Mattie was of Mi'kmaq/Montagnais Indian descent. He was a revered chieftain among his people. He had "royal" blood in his veins. His bloodline reached back into the realms of pre-recorded history. The tales of his breed had been passed down through long generations beside countless campfires in wonderfully told accounts by those who knew and who believed.

He was the descendant of an ancient nomadic people who had roamed the steppes of a far eastern land. The land bridge that had kept the earth's greatest land mass as one allowed his magnificent, wandering, fearless ancestors access to a land of wonders. In his veins coursed the blood of ageless corsairs for whom distant oceans were never a barrier. He was truly a man of the earth. He was timeless.

A brief rest slowed his pulsating blood as his wet clothing cooled him. Knowing he would get a chill with a prolonged stop, he moved away from the rim of the valley. A few long strides took him across a narrow meadow and to the edge of the dripping woods beyond.

He was about to enter a faint trace, his right hand lifting a snow-sodden alder branch out of his way, when a distant, muffled boom thudded up through the valley behind him. Mattie froze but didn't turn his head toward the sound. For several minutes he waited, listening for the sound to come again.

When it came again he turned, and before the sound had faded away he was standing once more on the valley edge. It had come from the direction of the sea just a few miles away to the west. Despite the high mountains with their deep valleys, there was no following echo from the loud noise, just a dull roar that hung for a while in the damp air before dissipating.

It was a ship's cannon fire. Mattie was as sure of that as if he had been standing on the coastline watching the white men play with their modern weapons. He had heard the sound many times before and had once been witness to a strange event involving the big black guns.

* * * * *

IT HAD BEEN A QUIET, WARM SUNDAY morning that summer past. Mattie had decided to attend Mass in his small village. The Catholic Church had always played a big part in the lives of his people. It was a friendship that had begun long before Mattie's time, across the water on the mainland of Canada.

The native peoples of that vast land to the westward had no say in the forced occupation of their country by warring nations of white men. The two nations that were the most vicious in their dominance of so much natural virgin wealth were the English and the French. These two neighbouring countries had fought against each other for centuries on the east side of the Atlantic and now sought to extend their battlefield. They came to lord over the land. They wanted the fish and the fur-bearing animals, the immense tracts of timber, the stretches of fertile land. It was an unimaginable resource to the land-hungry and resource-starved explorers from Europe. It was a land that knew nothing of the modern invention of steel.

The hook, the trap, and the gun would bring an ages-old native lifestyle to an end. The invading people with the sickly skin colour wanted to own the very land that the indigenous peoples had occupied forever. This was a concept the natives could not understand. How could anyone own the earth? It was under the feet of everyone. It was a part of all of their races. The magnificent waters running through it were like clear bloodlines that linked humans to the Great Spirit. The white man claimed ownership over the land that wasn't theirs to take in the first place.

The Mi'kmaq people of which Mattie Mitchell was a part would survive the wars, but would never be their own complete and unique nation again. Of the two foreign nations vying for dominance over the virgin continent, the Mi'kmaq aligned themselves with the French, and along with them their version of Catholicism.

Mattie knew about his people's belief in Glooscap, their god who came from nothing. According to their ancient belief, Glooscap was a man created from speech. Secretly, Mattie didn't see much difference in this belief than the Christian belief. He had never heard the priest say where God came from. He knew God had a son who came from a woman whom had never lain with a man and that this man and his father were supposed to be the same person. This same God blew His breath upon the dust of the land and created man. Mattie dared not mention the similarities between the two beliefs. For Mattie, to sit at the back of the church and experience the reverence of something he never quite understood was in itself spiritual.

Several wharves jutted out into the calm Sunday morning harbour, and as Mattie walked along he noticed a schooner was tied securely across the head of one of the wharves. Below her two masts, and fastened diagonally to them on the main- and fore booms, two stained brown sails were neatly furled. Docked as it was, the schooner and the rickety wharf had formed a T jutting from the craggy shoreline. Mattie had always liked the little schooners, though he had never sailed on one. Watching them sail in and out of the bays, sometimes seeing them below him as he stood atop a high fjord, they always seemed to be quick, spirited things, borne freely along by a brisk wind.

As he drew nearer to the schooner, several shouting men were hastening out onto the wharf toward it. The rickety wharf creaked and buckled under the feet of so many hurrying men. Mattie stopped at the wharf's entrance, and without venturing onto it, listened to the noisy white men.

"I tells 'e 'tis no good to be wasting a cannon shot yet. 'Twill take seven days fer a body to come afloat."

This shout came from a bearded, burly man who had just appeared through the slanted forecastle door. Judging by the way the rest of the men were looking to him for answers, Mattie guessed he was the schooner's skipper.

"Well, 'tis not shot we're asking 'e to fire from the bloody cannon. Only a charge of black powder, is all. An' I always heard 'twould take only three days fer a drownded body to come back up. An' 'tis been four days now since poor Walt disappeared."

The small, skinny man who was shouting his concerns into the captain's face seemed to be speaking for the rest of the crowd. They all yelled in support.

The church bell started to ring across the calm, black water. The men, some of them still standing on the wharf, some of them aboard the schooner, all turned as one toward the sound. Mattie stood with his hands in his pockets and continued watching. He was amused by the loud talk and wondered what would happen next. The ringing bell gave the captain what he thought could be a way out of shooting his cannon.

"B'ys, can't ya hear the bell ringing? 'Tis Sunday morning, fer gawd's sake. I can't be firing guns on Sunday morning."

"Don't let that bother you none. 'Tis only the first bell, and besides, that's a Catholic church. They got nothing against firing guns on Sunday. By the time the second bell rings out we can have it over with, an' not only that, who knows? Poor Walt could be brought up from the deep!"

The thin man was waving his arms at the skipper, pointing at the church and gesticulating out over the water at the same time. Mattie knew he was cursing at the schooner skipper. Cursing was something for which Mattie's ancient Mi'kmaq language had no words. He had asked a white man once what he meant by those cursing words. Most of them had been drawn from the Bible, but the man who was so vehemently uttering them could not explain them. Mattie observed they were usually said during bouts of anger or excitement.

The captain mumbled something that Mattie could not hear. Walking behind the tall mainmast of the schooner, the skipper stopped before a small bundle covered with a tarp. Pulling the heavy covering away from the pile, he exposed what appeared to be a tangle of manila and hemp ropes. It took him several minutes to reveal under the snarl of rope what indeed looked like a small cannon.

"This is not a man-o'-war but a fishing vessel. The old whale gun could come in handy if we are of a mind to shoot at one of the big ones sometime."

The captain seemed to be a bit self-conscious due to the size of his "ship's cannon" now exposed for all to see. Some of the men gathered around were taken aback by the small gun, but the skinny one who had the most lip was not.

"By gawd, 'tis not the size of the gun that matters but the bloody racket it can make. That's what we're after this marnin'. Poor Walt loved the sound of a loud gun, he did—'twill bring him up, fer sure."

Mattie looked on with interest. He knew what they were about to do. He had seen it done once before. From the few glazed streaks of paint left on the gun, it was obvious it had once been black. But now dark red blotches of rust dominated it's surface. Pitted metal sores ran the length of the small cannon barrel, so that it resembled a small cylinder of discarded metal more than it did a cannon.

Between the shouts and all the commotion around the schooner, Mattie learned that "poor Walt" had been missing for four days. It was also pointed out to the reluctant captain that he had last been seen walking along the shoreline long after dark and had not been seen since. *Stumbling along is more like it,* thought Mattie, who knew the missing man very well, but not by association. They were naming him right, he reasoned. Walt was a poor everything: a poor hunter and poor trapper as well as poor fisherman. The only time Walt was good at any of these things was when the bragging accounts coming from his drunken mouth drew a few unknowing listeners. Mattie also knew that Walt had been on a drinking binge this time for as many days as he had now been missing.

Apparently a woman had looked out into the night from behind her kitchen curtain before heading upstairs to her bed, and she had seen him staggering along the landwash. From her account and because he had not been seen for days, and after a brief search around the surrounding forest had shown not a trace of him, it was determined that Walt had fallen into the cold waters of the bay.

Mattie figured if he was in the water he could just as easily have been pushed in. Walt was known for his rowdiness when in his cups and would start fights that would seldom finish in his favour.

An order of "Stand clear!" was suddenly shouted from the schooner captain, who was standing over the whale gun with what appeared to be a burning stick in his hand. He held the burning end against a thin, dark fuse sticking up out of the back of the cannon. Just when it seemed it would not ignite, it sizzled into a smoky yellow flame that travelled down the twisted length of fuse and disappeared into the bore of the cannon. By now everyone, including the skipper, had jumped out over the gunnels of the schooner to stand on the creaking wharf. From the mouth of the cannon came a single perfect ring of smoke. From the small hole where the burning fuse had disappeared came a long *pftt!* sound like that of a fat squid on a jigger, and nothing more.

Everyone started yelling at the captain at once, blaming him for the "dud" shot. The captain yelled back, "It wasn't my fault! Maybe the bloody powder was damp!" He started to climb back aboard his schooner to check on the failed firing of the gun, when a blue, black, and white plume of smoke erupted from each end of the cannon. From the business end erupted a long, thin, yellow tongue of flame followed by an ear-splitting explosion that silenced the second church bell, which had just begun. The noise burst out over the still waters of the harbour, boomed way out the bay, and roared back from the hills. When the echo died, the next sounds came from every dog in the place. The barking that followed created almost as much disquiet as had the cannon. And, still, "poor Walt" did not appear.

High in the hills, wet and tired, Mattie Mitchell smiled at the memory. The sound he had heard just a few minutes before came again. This wasn't someone hoping to raise a dead body from the depths. Of that he was pretty sure. The sound did not come again. Striding once more into the dark forest, the tall Indian vanished from the mountain meadow.

* * * * *

DOWN OVER THE WHITE MOUNTAINS, through the wooded gorges, across the sloped, spring-flowing valleys and out into the ice-packed Gulf of St. Lawrence, a small schooner lay jammed solid. Dark figures scrambling down her shaky rope ladders and wooden side sticks jumped drunkenly onto the hummocky ice that held them prisoner. The first few steps the black-clad men took left dirty, grease-stained prints on the virgin ice: the filth from the schooner's deck trailing the hunters.

The schooner's white mainsail appeared to be new and was billowed full with a following wind. Her foresail was brown and showed many sewn patches, the stitching showing like the healed scabs from numerous wounds. This sail too was pulling with all of its strain. But still the schooner was not moving.

The vessel was leaning to starboard at an alarming angle and was in danger of being broached by the terrible pressure exerted on her port side by the squeezing ice. On board, the men flung heavy hemp lines from her bow and, on the ice, the others hurriedly gathered them up. Placing the ropes over their shoulders, and bent over like straining, hauling dogs, and bellowing some obscure seaman's shanty, the sealers pulled with all their might. Now the sails luffed a bit as the men shouted, the mast rigging creaked and clinked, the schooner yawed more to starboard and groaned her misery, but still she remained held in the frozen grip.

At a command from the schooner's skipper the ropes were discarded. The men hurried back along both sides of the hapless boat, where they stood and awaited further instructions. Two greasy poles about ten feet long were handed down over the sides of the schooner by the few men still on deck, along with several quart-sized cans of black powder. The two men who took the wooden poles quickly lashed one tin of the canned explosives to one end of each pile. Thin, black fuses no more than a foot long were attached to one end of the cans. Now the two men separated from the crowd. Running like proud warriors, their raised standards swaying as they went, they soon reached the bow of the stricken vessel.

As the seal hunters watched, the "powder men"—these young men had to be quick on their feet—knelt on the ice and tried to find a hole suitable to push the ends of the poles beneath the surface. It was a difficult task, and at first it seemed they would have to resort to axes to chop a hole in the pressing ice. They finally found a suitable opening between the tumbled ice pans and rammed the powder cans, their smoking lucifers already lit, below the ice until they disappeared with only the black tips of the blasting tips showing above the ice.

To the shouts of "Run, ya young buggers, run!" from the captain and excited yells from the watching men, the powder men raced back toward the ship, weaving around and jumping over the hummocks of ice. The shouting men fell suddenly silent when the two blasters reached them. For several seconds there was no sound at all. Then a deep, muffled rumble came from below the ice and, with a tumultuous *whump*, the exploding powder burst itself free of the ice. Pulverized snow and blue ice shot into the air and fell back like white chowder. Several thick, sheared ice pans rolled over, exposing their blue undersides.

A narrow black lead of water appeared. The sails bent. The schooner lurched ahead a few feet and tried to right itself, but then stopped again. A frantic yell from the schooner's deck sent the powder men racing back toward the vessel's straining bow again.

The process was repeated as before. A second blast bellowed upward, spending its energy among the tumbling ice pans. Another, wider lead of roiling water appeared. The schooner eagerly plunged its way into it, surging forward, seizing its chance for freedom. The men shouted in triumph and went running after the slow-moving schooner with its ropes trailing.

The explosion of sound roared away over the ice toward the nearby land, the second sound wave following the first up through a mountain gorge, to die at the very edge of a silent valley.

CHAPTER 3

PRESENTLY, MATTIE CAME UPON A SMALL, snow-covered clearing in the middle of the thick forest. At the north side of the clearing and nestled into the edge of the trees stood a rough wigwam with a south-facing skin door. The trees in the place had not been cut and the clearing seemed to be natural. There are many such in every forest. The white surface of a small pond showed beyond the trees, and behind the wigwam Mattie could hear more than see a small stream running toward the small body of water. Listening to the burble of the stream, he noted another sign of the fading winter. When he had left this place a week ago the brook was frozen and silent.

He stopped at the edge of the heavy trees to examine the wigwam. The structure blended in so completely with its surroundings that a furtive glance could very well have passed over it. It stood no more than ten feet wide at its circular base and its height ended in a narrow, conical shape about as high as the base was wide. Dozens of smooth, unpeeled, green aspen poles had long since been driven into the earth at an oblique angle. Their raised, axe-sharpened, crossed ends were blackened from countless campfires. This wooden skeleton was covered with overlapping layers of pale white birch bark that stopped short of the raised pole ends. Lodged over this bark layer and resting between each underlying pole were more poles of slender aspen holding the thin natural covering secure. The door was made from the hides of two or more stitched caribou quarters, the thick fur intact and laced at the top.

Nothing seemed disturbed and after a while Mattie stepped boldly across the clearing and approached the wigwam. When he released the heavy load from his tired shoulders and straightened his back, he staggered just a bit with the sudden relief from the day-long weight. The thump line left a reddish mark across his forehead. Wisps of steam that had been clinging to his wet woollen jacket beneath the loaded pack drifted away from the man as he stretched erect.

The door opened without a sound when he threw back the animal skin to reveal a black, oblong hole. He fastened the bottom end of the skin door above the opening. His frame filling the entrance, Mattie had to double over to step inside. Walking to the cold, grey ash firepit, he knelt down. Over time, the constant use of this fireplace had worn and burned a shallow hole in the earth, so that now it was below the level of the floor.

Taking some thinly crushed birch bark and dried yellow mosses, he laid them on a larger piece of birch placed on the dead ashes. He placed small twigs and then larger ones on top. Rising, he returned outside, picked up his pack with one hand, and walked back to the fireplace. From deep inside the pack he found a well-tied pouch, from which he removed a small wooden box. From inside it he drew a rectangular piece of steel and a dull grey, crescent-shaped piece of chert.

Creating a small hole inside the crushed starter pile and with the steel in his right hand, Mattie made a sudden, rapid scrape against the sharp edge of the chert. He was rewarded with an instant spray of yellow sparks, which fell among the waiting fire starter. Bending over the smouldering tinder, he blew a long, soft breath. The glow became a flaring burst of fire. He carefully placed the nest of the prepared kindling over it and watched as it smoked, then blazed into life. And as simple as that, Mattie had a warm campfire going.

The smoke milled around the fire just above floor level at first, but as the heat increased, the smoke spiralled upward, until it slowed and sought an exit around the blackened poles. The fire snopped and burned steadily. Now the new light flickered along the inward-slanting walls of the wigwam. Shadows appeared where there had been none before.

As Mattie rose away from the fire, his silhouette preceded him, reaching like a stealthy apparition to the height of the dwelling. Just above his head and turning slowly on their tethers with the rising heat were several large, smoke-cured trout, as well as the remains of two half-eaten smoked salmon.

Reaching up with his knife, Mattie cut a large piece from one of the trout and chewed the reddish-brown flesh. He was starved. Opposite the trout and hanging without turning were the remains of a hindquarter of caribou meat. It too had been cured over time by campfire smoke, its outer skin crusted to a deep, leathery brown.

While relishing the taste of the smoked trout, Mattie cut a piece from the caribou haunch. The inner meat was a succulent pink and he cut away a generous portion. Sitting beside the fire with his knees raised, the tall Indian's silent form on the wall made only slight motions as his hand brought pieces of meat and fish to his mouth.

Stacked neatly near the doorway was a high cache of cured animal skins. Placed on the very top and with its eyeless head and tufted black ear tips facing the fire was the rich, silver-brown hide of a lynx. Its skin was spread-eagled over the pile of hides, its stumpy, black-tipped tail dangling over the edge of the stack. Above the hides and hanging from several of the rafter poles all around were an array of steel traps with fierce-looking teeth.

Opposite the furs and nearer the fire was a narrow raised sleeping mat. It was made entirely from the soft ends of green fir boughs that had faded a bit. The natural mattress was stitched and interlaced skilfully with the rich-smelling boughs. A heavy blanket sewed entirely from the hides of several caribou and with the outer hair still intact was folded on one end of the sleeping mat.

The simple, raw dwelling place smelled of leather hides and an unmistakably animal scent, earthy odours from the warm dirt floor, the rich, cured meat and fish, and fire smells of wood and heat. The place had a smell of warmth. The smell was a natural human-animal blend.

His hasty snack finished, his belly satiated but not full, Mattie stepped outside again and brought the beaver carcass back inside with him. With some difficulty he passed a string through the beaver's rictus teeth and tied the animal with its broad tail hanging down from the sloping rafters. Now began a skinning style that was unique to Mattie alone.

It was the same careful method of cutting he would use to paunch a fat caribou. Two fingers of his left hand kept the stomach entrails away from the opened stomach liner. He made an incision just above the animal's tail and pushed two of the inverted fingers of his left hand inside the cut. Holding the knife in his right hand, he inserted it, cutting edge up, between the two long fingers.

With his fingers keeping the point of the sharp knife away from the animal's stinking gut, he pushed the knife with one long, even stroke to the tip of its lower gaping jaw. With amazing speed and dexterity and without once cutting the valuable skin, Mattie soon had the big rodent free of its tawny pelt and slowly twisting on its noose. With efficient movements he gingerly cut at the base of the animal's wide tail to remove the tiny, yellowish green castor sack, making sure not to puncture the fetid voile. He placed the scent gland inside a small, thick leather bag he used for this purpose alone, secured the opening carefully, and set it aside.

With the naked beaver in hand he bent through the narrow opening and stepped out into the drizzly dusk, where no shadow followed him. He walked to the icy edge of the murmuring stream, placed the beaver, tail first, into the swift, black water, and laid open its distended belly with one swift cut. He pushed his fingers inside and with one fluid motion pulled the creature's bowels, stomach, and intestines free.

He threw all of it into the shallow brook and watched the pale viscera, floating down-tide, looking like several eels swimming in the dark water. The unwanted contents discarded, he tore the membrane that hung below the rib cage and ripped out the plump heart and viscous liver. After cleaning and rinsing the carcass in the cold water, Mattie stood erect in the dark night.

The narrow brook that came out of the thick forest hastened gaily toward the pond, its flow an oily black as it sped along the snow-white banks. A long, deep rumble came from the direction of the pond. Mattie, beaver in hand, turned toward the sound and listened. The noise came again and again. It was the deep groan of the ice slowly releasing its wintry grip on the pond. It was another sure sign of mild weather close by.

Somewhere behind him and coming from high up in the heavy woods, an owl sounded at regular intervals. Its cry was a sound not usually heard on a cold winter night. The great horned bird hooted again, sounding as if it were far away, though Mattie could tell it was near. The day, and now the night, showed all the signs of approaching warmth. His instinct told him this wasn't going to be like one of the midwinter mild spells. This was the beginning of spring. Maybe it was time to leave the mountains, he thought.

Back inside the wigwam, he hung the beaver up again. He placed a heavy, black iron skillet on top of the fire. From the beaver carcass he cut several strips of yellow fat. When he lodged the fatty strips inside the pan, they sizzled and slid around, greasing the surface. When the fat started to curl and smoke, its juices rendered, Mattie added the cut sections of tender heart muscle. He waited until the meat simmered before turning it over with his knife, then placed the soft liver in the pan. Savouring the rising steamy smell, he sat back and waited for his meal to cook. He wished he had a little salt left to flavour the meat.

His rich-smelling supper cooked, he carefully removed the hot pan from the fire. Spearing the meat with his knife, he ate the contents of the pan. His appetite appeased, Mattie returned the pan to its hook just above the floor and sat back again. Watching the pan, he waited.

From the upended pan, dark drops of grease fell onto a flat piece of wood. The drops slowed as the pan cooled and the heavy fat congealed on the wood. Before long a small, furry form appeared from the shadows. The tiny creature was below the light from the fire and created no shadow.

But when it stood on its hind legs and reached up to catch the grease dropping from the edge of the pan, the shadow of its head appeared on the birch wall. The Indian smiled, his even teeth showing white against his dark face. The grey field mouse looked plump and short on the ground, its bosom full and proud. It thinned and lengthened as it stretched upward for the tasty treat. The fat dripped, slowed, and then stopped. The tiny, patient mouse licked them all, while the quiet man watched. The fire crackled. A flaw of wind rustled a loose flap of bark on the outside wall. The owl hooted in the distance. The sounds of the running brook rose and fell with the wet night wind. Mattie Mitchell dozed in pure comfort, his head nodding.

The mouse started gnawing at the pungent fat that had collected on the piece of wood. The sound of its chewing brought Mattie fully awake. The sudden motion from the still human startled the mouse from its meal, but it didn't run away. It just hunched itself into a ball and, satisfied that it had made itself look impressively big and threatening, squeaked once. Soon the night visitor finished its treat and simply disappeared into the shadows at the base of the wigwam.

Rising now that his entertainment was over, Mattie stepped outside, yawning as he went. The misty rain had stopped and the woods dripped. He could hear the rustle of wet snow settling. The pond ice boomed and cracked as before. A wisp of grey-blue smoke with a few trailing yellow flankers rose soundlessly from the wigwam.

The wind from the southwest felt warm and soft on his skin. He walked behind his shelter, breaking through the snow in several places as he went. He stopped, looked up at the dark sky, and urinated. All the signs told him it was nearly time to leave. Mattie made up his mind quickly. After the next night frost, which was sure to come, he would leave the hills and make his way homeward, pulling his winter-caught furs behind him.

Returning to the wigwam, Mattie loosed the thong that held the door in place. The leather door fell and covered the hole completely behind him as he entered. He added a few more pieces of seasoned birch wood to his fire, then removed his damp coat and hung it to one of the rafters. Without removing any other article of clothing, not even his long leather boots, he lay down on his bunk.

The thick caribou blanket crackled as he pulled it up over his body. Mattie turned his back to the smouldering fire and settled his head into the fragrant pillow of fir boughs. Almost as soon as he had lain down, the long, blanket-covered figure was still. The fire flickered, casting unmoving shadows, and for a second a small flare from the fire glinted across the shiny black hair of the sleeping Indian.

Outside, the night aged; the wind died away; the clouds opened, revealing a profusion of twinkling stars; the sound of a single, lonely howl from a faraway prowling wolf came on the fading night wind. But aside from the sleeping meadow, its solitary plea was heard by no one.

* * * * *

EARLY IN THE CHRISTMAS MONTH of the year past, heavy frost and snow had finally come. It was the last few days of the year 1899. A new century was about to begin, an event that appeared to be of great consequence to the white people of Mattie's small village in the Bay of Islands. It was the start of a new modern era. Some of them were afraid. It would be the end of the world, they said. Many of the self-righteous religious ones spent their "last days" quoting Bible verses that supposedly verified their alarmist thinking.

To Mattie, who didn't own a calendar but measured his days and seasons by his wandering way of life, it was the end of nothing. It was just the beginning of another wonderful winter of trapping. Mattie always carried with him a brown, pocket-sized Catholic prayer book that had been translated into his native Mi'kmaq language. Mattie was literate enough to read portions of it. Nowhere in his cherished book could he find a date for such a foolish portent.

He had spent the short, glorious days of autumn trapping

and hunting along the many rugged coves and coastal plains and tidal river valleys. The English demand for fancy beaver-skin hats had taken its toll on the animals all along the coast. Mattie would trap them on his winter trapline far inland, where few others went.

A big part of his fall trapping along the coast was for otter. Their rich autumn pelts were in good demand, but around the windy coast they were harder to trap than they were in the rivers and ponds. The otters that frequented the saltwater bays and inlets were usually much larger than the freshwater variety and fetched a better price when cured just right. Mattie used a short piece of net obtained from a fisherman friend of his, with which he netted herring for bait to trap the otters.

He was paddling along the shoreline in the middle of the afternoon. The day had been too windy to chance paddling along the cliffs that bordered the water. He had spent the time picking ripened berries that grew on every bank above the tide line. He had taken a good nap, too, with the cool breeze from the ocean rustling the low bushes all around the place where he had lain.

Now with the wind dropping and showing every indication of dying, he set off in his canoe. His net had been set yesterday just around the bill of the point he was now approaching. When he paddled around the point, he saw the shorefast net running down to the water and the small wooden buoy bobbing at the outside end of the net, but not one of the cork floats between shore and buoy could be seen.

At first he thought a whale had become entangled in the net—a minke or a pothead, maybe. He rested his paddle on the narrow gunnel and waited. The imagined whale never surfaced and, upon considering, Mattie figured one of these small whales could have parted the mooring lines and swam off still entangled in the netting.

He approached the net and, looking down into the depths, saw what had dragged the floats under. From the foot-ropes to the head yarkins the net was filled with silvery herring. Their combined weight was too much for the cork floats to bear. Many of the fish were still alive, and wriggled and twisted to free themselves from the narrow meshes. Their struggling caused thousands of shiny scales to break free and float away on the current, flashing and glistening, only to vanish into the green depths.

The dead ones hung limp and motionless. Yellow, short-legged crab, and pink and green starfish with five fingers spread, were feasting on them. Below the net, wide-mouthed sculpins and squished-mouthed flatfish, their black eyes looking up, waited for the carrion.

Mattie had seen nets sunk with herring before. It was a common thing for the fishermen along this coast to witness. The schooling herring swam along these waters by the tons, both in the spring and fall. Mattie had seen them in the mouths of streams, with the milky sperm from the males clouding the tidal pools for days. At such times it was easy to scoop up hundreds of the fish by hand or with dipnets.

Mattie suddenly remembered another time when a small section of his net had been carried under, and it wasn't by herring. An otter had been chasing herring and its paws had become twisted in the mesh. Its frantic struggle for life had only entangled the animal more. Mattie found the drowned otter hopelessly rolled in the linnet a few feet below the surface. Looking down at the hundreds of herring and remembering the otter, he had an idea.

He knew where to find several otter slides, where the playful animals slid down over the rocks into the sea. Favourite slides were used by the same otter families for years. In such places the otters created a muddy run from treeline to the ocean edge. The muddy "rub" or "burry" was their giveaway to knowing trappers.

Placed upon the rocks well above the surf line, and near the place where Mitchell had fastened his net to the land, were several lobster pots. Many of the local fishermen, instead of freighting their pots up the long bays to home after the season's fishing, simply carried them ashore to a convenient site. It was on this very coast where Mattie had seen his very first lobster trap around the year 1870. At that time he wasn't sure what he was seeing. But by 1873, a small lobster canning factory was started by a Nova Scotia man and the handmade wooden traps or pots were a common sight. By 1888 the fishery had expanded until the English had established more than two dozen such factories along this coast, and Mattie knew where a lone Frenchman had one. Mattie's quick mind soon had figured a unique way of trapping the otters. He would combine their love for chasing and eating herring—with a lobster pot!

It took him a while to raise a part of the submerged net and take from it several dozen herring before letting it sink to the bottom again. It was a delicate task while sitting in the stern of a shallow, narrow canoe. There was a danger of capsizing it, but after he had wrangled a portion of the net across the centre of the craft, the canoe was held steady with the net's weight. He simply shook the net until all the herring he wanted fell aboard.

He gingerly manoeuvred the glistening net back over the bow of the canoe and, paddling to shore, stepped out. Climbing the sloping, sea-smoothed cliff, he knelt beside the neatly stacked lobster pots and considered his plan. Several pots had been discarded next to the stored ones. They had been damaged by wave and prolonged use and were badly in need of repair. They would do nicely.

The pots were close to three feet long and had two bent spruce saplings on either end and one in the middle, fastened to the bottom frame, giving the pot an oval shape. Both ends and sides had separate lathes nailed to them. Inside the "parlour" was fastened a sharpened "bait stick." The working side of the pots had tube-shaped netting for the lobster to enter, as well as a small, easily removable door to retrieve them.

Deciding to use just one pot for his experiment, Mattie removed part of the head or end of the pot and, using his axe and knife, had soon fashioned a hole of nine to ten inches across between the lathes. He secured one of his wire snares across the opening and, with the pot loaded into the centre of his canoe, paddled his way along the shoreline.

The wind had dropped away to a mere breeze. Black shadows reached away from the high land. The canoe's faint wake left a silvery crease in the water as it passed. An eagle perched atop one of the tall trees eyed the herring in the canoe out of its reach.

Mattie picked up one of the herring and gave it a throw. The eagle left its lofty perch as soon as the fish splashed into the water. The bird soared on silent wings toward the herring, dived, and stretched its mighty yellow talons toward the sinking fish. It tried its best, but sped away from the water with naked claws. The herring had sunk before the eagle reached it.

Picking up another herring, Mattie threw it as high as he could. The fish shone and twisted and turned in a long arc over the black water. The watching eagle dived again. There was a swishing sound when its feet brushed the water. Without once flapping its broad wings, it soared skyward again. Shiny water droplets fell away as it rose with the silver herring firmly gripped between one of its claws.

Mattie could smell the otter rub before he reached it. The strong scent of the animals had permeated into the damp soil where they played. He stopped paddling and let the boat drift to the water's edge below the rub. There were no otters to be seen anywhere, but the rub was dark and wet. Showing below the mudslide and traced across the smooth cliff, just above where the ocean quietly lapped upon the rocks, was a damp water trail. At least one otter had been here recently.

Mattie skivvered three of the biggest herring onto the bait stick inside the lobster pot, lifted the pot carefully out of his canoe, and placed it into the water. He lowered the pot slowly with the buoy rope and watched as it sank in the clear water. He tugged it a couple of times to make sure it rested level on the bottom just below the otter slide. When it was down and to his liking he threw the line overboard with the small, wooden, tapered buoy fastened to one end.

Just before dark, he paddled into a tiny cove where a small brook ran through a narrow, crescent-shaped beach. He pulled his canoe well above the surf line, got a fire going using pieces of driftwood, placed his flat-bottom kettle over it to boil, and began cleaning a meal of herring for his supper.

The following morning, before the wind came to the bay, Mattie paddled to where the lone lobster buoy tugged and bobbed on the tide. He reached for the buoy and, pulling in the slack, was soon directly over the sunken trap. He peered down and was surprised to see the dark brown body of a dead otter lying half in and half out of the lobster pot. His trap had worked perfectly. Over the next few days he pulled eleven otters from four lobster pots all carefully placed in the water below a fresh otter burry. When he returned home with the eleven pelts he was asked how he had done so well in such a short time. Mattie Mitchell simply replied, with an air of mystery, "I jest use ol' Indian trick."

CHAPTER 4

MATTIE LEFT THE COAST WHEN THE NIGHTS turned cold and the frost came. He headed for the long, sloping hills and the high mountain valleys beyond. These were the places he truly loved best. He had prolonged his winter trapline trip to correspond with the right travelling conditions.

Before he had reached all the way into the high country beyond Bonne Bay, he realized he had waited too long. The snows were much deeper here, and before the first day of hard walking was through he had donned his homemade snowshoes. All of the belongings he would need for the entire winter were towed behind him on a small wooden sled, or carried on his broad shoulders in a packsack.

He spent the first night in a makeshift shelter that he had built just before the early dark, and dozed through the long winter night beside a small fire he kept burning. The second night he sheltered in a temporary tilt situated along his trapline route. The close of the third snowy day found him at the door of his wigwam.

The spoor of game was not as prevalent along the way as he had hoped. In the coastal valleys he had left behind, many of the white settlers were augmenting their lean summer fishing with fur trapping. But few white men came here to the mountains. Many of the places he trapped were exclusive to him alone. He seldom saw anyone, Indian or white. Still, from his observations along the way, good signs of the fur-bearing animals he hunted and trapped were scarce.

From his pack and sled he carried the scanty provisions inside his winter teepee. A small bag of tea—which wouldn't last him the winter—and a smaller bag of coarse sugar, along with a quart tin of blackstrap molasses, he put inside and hung from the rafter poles. These three items, he knew, would be used up first. It was his one weakness for the white man's food: Mattie Mitchell had a sweet tooth. About fifteen pounds of flour and a small bag of pale white salt crystals that would need some crushing completed his supply.

As was his wont, Mattie patrolled around his immediate camping area the very next morning. He was eager to scout around the outlying valleys and hills. He travelled along on snowshoes over the virgin snow. Down each hidden forest glade and unmarked trace he stepped joyfully along.

In his left hand he carried a long-barrelled Martin Henry rifle that had seen much use. In his pocket were four brass bullets for the gun. They were the only ammunition he owned. In his right hand he held a sharp axe that he frequently swung at low-hanging limbs that were in his way. He paid careful attention to every detail as if he were seeing it all for the first time.

He was crossing a small stream. Its snowy banks, now well above the running water, indicated that over the years it had been well used to a deeper, swifter flow. Directly across the brook from him was a recently foundered gravel bank that the slowly moving water had only partly washed away. When the cut-bank had occurred, probably during last spring's melt, it had exposed a large, brown, rust-stained, jutting outcrop of rock, its base not yet washed clean by the low water levels of the stream. For years Mattie had used this stream for crossing. He had not seen the rock formation before.

The different and out of the ordinary always drew his eye. He crossed the brook in a few quick strides, the frigid water leaving a wet mark halfway up the calf of his leather boots. Standing at the base of the jagged cliff, Mattie tried to understand what it was he was seeing and immediately knew where he had seen it before.

* * * * *

IT WAS DURING HIS TIME SPENT GUIDING for the Newfoundland-born geologist James Patrick Howley and Howley's mentor, Scottish-born Alexander Murray. Both men treated Mattie with respect. Just three years Mattie's junior, Howley treated him as an equal.

Howley held Mattie Mitchell in such high esteem as to recommend his delightful Indian guide to the Newfoundland government as the finest of men and the best of guides. Mattie called Howley "Sage," the Mi'kmaq word for James. James Howley always called Mattie "Matthieu."

Mattie had been a single young man of twenty in 1864, yet his remarkable skills and wilderness knowledge were well-known, from the tiny villages of Halls Bay on the northeast coast of the island to the mountain fjords of the west coast. Murray and Howley were in the employ of the Newfoundland government to determine and document the island's resources.

The last time any serious inquiry into the natural resources of this, tenth of the world's largest islands, had been done was back in 1839, when the geologist Joseph Beete Jukes had done preliminary work here. Jukes had primarily conducted coastal surveys with few forays into what the white men considered—

because they hadn't ventured there—the "fearful" wilderness of this remarkable island.

One of the few interior expeditions Jukes did make was up the mouth of the smooth Humber River as far as the long, narrow Deer Lake. This had been a relatively easy exploratory excursion for the geologist. It had been made all that much easier by the expert guiding skills provided by the west coast Mi'kmaq Indians which Jukes seldom named.

Murray and his eager protege, Howley, would do more than explore the coastal regions of this unique North Atlantic nation. They were tasked by the government, and quite willingly intended, to traverse as much of the landscape as possible, including the hinterland. They loved their job. It would take the two paid pioneers many years of diligent, meticulously documented surveying, and even then they had only skimmed a few places of the vast interior of this intricate island.

Alexander Murray was a geologist born on June 2, 1810, in "Dollierie House," Crieff, Scotland. He was the very first director of the Geological Survey of Newfoundland. He came to the island in 1864 and was enthralled with all of its largely unspoiled, unexplored—at least by the white population— territory. It was as much unlike his country as it was possible to be. Murray stayed here until 1884, when he returned to Scotland. He died in Belmont Cottage in Crieff, Scotland, the following year at the age of seventy-four.

Mattie Mitchell, at twenty-two years of age, met the fifty-six-year-old Murray in 1866. They were joined by Newfoundland's own geologist, James Howley, two years later. The two geologists would walk the hills, scale the cliffs, walk and sometimes float downstream, and make their difficult way against river currents for more than twenty years. And guiding them on all of their major forays was the Indian Mattie Mitchell.

Up the Indian River from Halls Bay he led them in the month of June, when the flies feed in swarms. Or, as Murray put it: "The black buggers have voracious apatite, and tek a mon's bluid so that I wonder the greate horrads of them aire not redd."

South, and away from the waters that run east into the Notre Dame Bay, Mitchell led them to the west- and south-running waters of the huge Humber River system, which pours into the Bay of Islands on Newfoundland's west coast. Murray and Howley kept carefully written records and mapped their expeditions. They took note of great tracts of timber that took days to walk through, and the rivers to get them to potential sawmills and markets. They noted powerful waterfalls and deep waters, and fish stocks as well as their spawning beds. The explorers came upon veins of coal, copper, lead, zinc, and traces of gold. The host rocks of the minerals, and in come cases their compass bearings, were entered accurately into their well-thumbed ledgers.

They talked about their findings as they wrote them down at the end of every long day. The men showed Mattie how to identify minerals, realizing early on that his incredible eye for detail was a valued asset with their work. They showed him what to look for and told him, "Rocks never rust. Only metals rust." And always their tall, quiet guide listened and would forever remember.

Mattie held the Scotsman in high regard and some reverence. At almost every evening meal, Murray would clasp his hands together, bow his head, and say the grace of Scotland's greatest bard, Robert Burns: "Some hae meat and cannae eat, some would eat that want it, but we hae meat and we can eat, sae let the Lord be thankit." And when he finished, Mattie always said "Amen."

Mattie also considered Alexander Murray to be the toughest white man he knew, and with good reason.

They were working in the Cape St. George area of the Port au Port peninsula. Murray was doing his usual detailed mapping of every brook he found and recording the potential resources. They had been in the area for a few days and had walked the entire sandy length of Long Point. Standing alone at its naked northernmost point, with a brisk summer wind rising from the gulf with the evening tide, Murray breathed deep of the sea air and quoted his beloved Robert Burns again: "Nae man can tether time or tide."

That next morning, it rained. They were making their sodden way to the narrow isthmus of the small peninsula late that evening, where they planned to spend the night. The men were hurrying, longing to get there. They had crossed it on the way out and had left their camp there in the east bay for their return.

It was a magical place, surrounded by beaches, filled with seasoned grey driftwood that washed ashore from the huge western gulf. It made the best firewood. With hundreds of nesting waterfowl flying in from both the Port au Port and St. George's Bay sides, they would dine on roasted duck tonight.

It was their haste over the wet ground that took Murray down. Keeping pace with Mattie's long steps ahead of him, Murray jammed his right foot into a rock crevice at the very extent of its back reach. When he pulled the leg, without breaking his stride, his anchored foot yanked him back like a spring. He fell forward, twisting sideways as he went down. When his crushing weight fell upon the twisted leg bone, his fibula cracked and he tore his Achilles tendon.

The scream of pain that escaped the man's clenched teeth stopped Mattie in his tracks. He rushed to Murray's side. Murray was lying half on his side and half on his back, with both hands clasping his lower leg. His hat had come off. His packsack had shifted up over his round shoulders during the fall. He leaned his balding head back upon it, wincing in pain.

His foot was still wedged between the rocks. Seeing what

had to be done, Mattie helped Murray to his feet and pulled his foot back, freeing him. Murray's face was flushed. His foot burned like fire. Sweat appeared on the cheekbones above his bearded jaws and beaded on his rain-soaked skin. He felt dizzy and staggered against Mattie's chest. He thought he was going to faint, but the nauseous wave passed and he stood on one foot with an arm around Mattie's shoulder.

Murray knew he was in trouble. They were days away from any medical assistance. He wasn't even sure if there was a doctor on the coast. Mattie helped him to their camp and laid him down upon his blanket inside the tent. When he removed Murray's trousers, he discovered his leg was terribly bruised and badly swollen. After starting a fire outside their camp, Mattie quickly walked away in the damp evening.

When he returned, he had in his hands a clump of moist black mud wrapped in thin, greenish yellow fronds of kelp. When he gently smeared the cooling mud over Murray's swollen leg, the man sighed in instant relief and thanked him. Mattie covered the mud-encased lower leg and ankle with the wet, salty kelp. He used a piece of the kelp "belt" and tied it around the bandage to hold it all in place. That night, Murray sat framed by the firelight in the tent flap and entered his day's work in his ledger.

With a fire going outside their camp, the men discussed their options. An overland route to any of the settlements that might offer medical assistance was out of the question. Murray couldn't walk, and for Mattie to carry him would only add to his agony. Mattie figured they should try and get a boat and sail either north to the Bay of Islands, or across St. George's Bay and south to Port aux Basques.

But the stubborn Murray would hear none of it. They would only get him to a doctor who would do little more than "administer their foule tasting concoctions. I weel go nowhaire," he said.

While the Scotsman mended, Mattie gathered eggs from the nesting seabirds. After boiling them, he soaked them in sea water overnight. They would last for days. He caught trout in the streams and speared flatfish in the shallow waters. He killed waterfowl with his bow and arrow. Once, Murray watched as he brought down a curious, slow-flying herring gull with one arrow. Mattie skinned the bird and, that evening, after he roasted it with two other seabirds, Murray couldn't taste the difference between the seagull and the others.

Murray was on his feet again in two days and, with the support of a crutch made by Mattie, started to hobble his way along. And with all of his pain, Murray never once complained or asked for favours from the other man.

He never did seek medical attention for his ailment and continued with his work for years afterward. But for the rest of his life Alexander Murray walked with a limp. After his injury, Murray was offered and gladly accepted the services of Newfoundland-born geologist James Howley.

* * * * *

JAMES PATRICK HOWLEY WAS BORN IN St. John's on July 7, 1847. He was a geologist by profession, but as his work with Murray progressed, he became an excellent surveyor. Using his carefully described entries recorded in the field by the light of a smoky lantern and flickering campfire, he also added "Author" as another of his titles. Howley was Murray's protégé. Murray was Howley's mentor.

Howley was always a very kind and devout man, courteous, easygoing, and generally a very pleasant man to be around. He was uncommonly strong, and walked tirelessly, or, as Mattie put it with a grin, "Sage ver' strong man. Almos' strong as me, maybe. 'E walk my walk, too." Howley and Mattie Mitchell became good friends and remained together long after Murray had gone back to his native Scotland.

Howley followed Mattie and trusted the man's amazing instinct. The geologist used other guides in his travels but could find no one to be Mattie's equal. He relied on him exclusively whenever it was possible to avail of the Indian's services.

The two men travelled and explored all along the snarl of coves and bays and narrow inlets of the Connaigre peninsula on Newfoundland's rugged south coast. Mattie led the intrepid geologist around Hermitage Bay to Gaultois Island, where the Mi'kmaq people had found refuge from the French and English wars hundreds of years before.

At every night's campfire, James Howley did his best to teach Mattie Mitchell the mysteries of science. In turn, Mattie told Howley the ways of his people handed down to him from a thousand such night fires. And Howley always listened.

With Mattie, Howley paddled in wonderment the length of the huge glacial fjord of Bay d'Espoir. When they arrived at its farthest reach into insular Newfoundland, the two stayed for a time at the Mi'kmaq village of Miawpukek, or Conne River, where Howley updated his maps.

They were sitting by their campfire just above a gravelly beach on their last night in the hamlet. The sea was calm here in this deep bay. The water looked like a calm, black pond and not at all like the tormented waters of the Atlantic.

Howley was entering detailed accounts of his travels into his ledger. He frequently wetted the black tip of his pencil between his lips before each entry. Pausing in his work, he looked across the bright fire at Mattie and asked him how it was that he could keep everything so precise in his mind.

"I don't mean the bays themselves. Anyone can remember

big items. What I mean is your keen knowledge of every rock and shoal and hidden reef on salt water or fresh water, for not only this coast, but for every coast we have travelled."

"Don't know why," said Mattie. "Ever' place I bin stay in my min' ver' easy."

Howley bent over his precious book again and turned it to get better light on the page. "You know, Matthieu, there was an English hydrographer by the name of Captain James Cook who mapped this coast hundreds of years ago. I wonder if he too had a Mi'kmaq man to guide his ship around this coast of so many treacherous bays."

Mattie was looking at the black runnels of quiet night water as they ran along the edge of the beach and didn't answer for a moment. Then he asked in his quiet way, "'E da same captain man who cut ears from 'is sailors wit' long knife?"

Howley dropped his pencil in astonishment at the question. He dragged the long fingers of one hand through his scraggly beard and drew the other hand over his balding white head. It was a move Mattie recognized as one Howley made whenever he was excited or upset.

Cook was the greatest of all explorers. He was the best of navigators, and cartographer extraordinaire. He had sailed the world over claiming many firsts for a European. He was stabbed to death in the Hawaiian Islands by a Hawaiian chieftain while trying to take their king hostage.

One of Cook's well-known punishments for disobedience—something he would not abide—was to order one of the ears to be cut from the offending crew member. Despite his sadistic method of maiming as a form of punishment, Howley was one of Cook's greatest admirers.

"How do you know of this, Matthieu?" Howley asked incredulously. "You could not possibly have read it!"

Despite Howley's obvious excitement, Mattie paused before answering, as was his way. When he spoke again his voice was calm and matter-of-fact. "Dere is ol' tale tol' by my people of ver' pale-skinned captain man. Dey talk dis man ver' long time ago. Dis man 'ave no 'air on 'is face. 'E come 'ere in great ship wit' t'ree spars. One time his man flee to our lan'. When captain man fin' him 'e cut 'is ear off wit' long knife an' t'row in salt sea."

Howley was speechless for a long time, something that was unusual for him. When he spoke again he had resumed his calm demeanour. "Matthieu, I sometimes doubt the words of your oral history. Yet I wonder about the volumes that will forever remain hidden."

They talked then of the long wilderness that lay ahead of them, of rivers and lakes they would have to cross. And again Howley wondered how it was that Mattie could know such an immense area so intimately. He asked Mattie if all of his people were as adept and knowledgeable with wilderness lore as he. Mattie stirred the fire with a long, blackened stick before answering. Flankers rose on invisible heat waves and the fire flared up, casting shimmering yellow streaks out over the limpid water.

"Ver' many my people good trapper. Some not so good. One man live east on Akilasiye'wa'kik Quospem. The white man call dis place Gander Lake. 'Is name Soulis Joe. We meet sometime on long trail. Talk trail talk. 'E ver' good man. Trap alone like me. Tall like me, too. Good as me, too—almos'." Mattie finished with a grin.

They left Miawpupek in the grey dawning of the next morning and crossed the southeast arm of the bay in a borrowed canoe. Mattie led the way, on familiar ground, to where Bay d'Espoir reached farthest inland. They walked northeast, skirting the southern banks of the many-angled Jeddore Lake, and camped by the water the Mi'kmaq called Ahwachanjeesh Pond.

Late one evening, from atop Mount Gabriel, Mattie pointed out the Annieopsquotch Mountains away to the west, a name his people used for "Terrible Rocks." He showed Howley the direction they would follow in the morning toward the high Ebbegunbaeg Hill. It was a landmark his people had followed across the land for years.

That night they camped in the shadow of Ebbegunbaeg, beside a stream that ran merrily along while the two weary travellers slept. They left in the morning with Ebbegunbaeg to their backs and walked west to Meelpaeg Lake, where they explored its eastern banks for two days.

Resuming their journey, they rounded the north end of Meelpaeg Lake and left the waters to continue their southerly flow behind them. From there they set out north and then east and followed the waterway to Noel Paul's Brook—named after another Mi'kmaq trapper—into Newfoundland's mightiest of rivers, the Exploits.

* * * * *

JAMES HOWLEY HAD COME BY SCHOONER to the Bay of Exploits in 1875, when he met with Mattie where the mighty Exploits River runs into the salt sea at Sandy Point.

Across the remotest parts of the island, Howley followed the Indian where few white men had ever walked before. It was the longest and most rewarding trek of his geological career. And when they walked out to the coast on the other side of the island, the two men were friends.

The two men set out in the heat of the summer midday on July 3. With Mattie leading the way and with Howley sketching and scribing his maps, they travelled north and west and finally south.

They walked along the Exploits waterway, where the Red
Indians came no more. They rafted rivers and ponds and camped
in the short summer nights to rest. On one such night they
were sitting on a wide beach next to a bright campfire on the
western shores of what Mattie called "The Red Pond." On this
rare occasion he asked Howley a question. "How come ever'one
call us Red Indians? No Red Indian 'ere no more. My skin eart'
colour, not red. We are people of de eart'."

And so, Howley, who knew much about history and who
had learned more from Mattie Mitchell than he could ever repay,
explained to Mattie how the native Indians of Newfoundland had
come to be called Red Indians. The Europeans, he told him, were
forever after the wealth of the eastern countries. The English and
French, the Spanish Conquistadores, and the Portuguese all sought
the spices and silks and rare jewels of far-off India and Asia. A
journey south past the great bulge of Africa and then east into
the Indian Ocean and beyond sometimes took years to complete.
When it became accepted that the earth was actually round—and
not flat, as most explorers of that day had believed—navigators
believed they could reach the eastern countries by sailing west.

Mattie frowned as he stirred the fire. He squinted in
concentration at this statement from Sage, but he remained quiet.
Howley continued.

"So they sailed west. And they came to this island. Some say
it took them thirty days to get here, some say it was more like
fifty days. In any case it was a far cry from a year's sailing. They
thought for sure they were in India!

"There are even tales of a fierce northern race of seafarers
who came here in long boats with high prows. But they are only
legends handed down and probably not to be believed."

Howley never noticed the strange look that came over
Mattie's face as he said this. Howley, reclining comfortably on

the sandy beach, sat up straight as he considered how best to relate the "discovery" of this island to his friend. Staring into their campfire, he went on.

"When they 'hove to' in their rolling caravels in some sheltered cove, somewhere around this island, they found there were already people living here. The Europeans called them Indians, and because their skin was painted red, they called them Red Indians."

Mattie was staring at Howley as he spoke. His face was a mask of concentration. Howley could see the man's intelligence as he digested what he was hearing.

"You know what is amazing, Matthieu? Even when these early explorers sailed thousands of miles farther south, they still figured they were in the Indies. They even called islands there the 'West Indies.' But what is more incredible is this. They gave the name 'Red Indians' to all of the native peoples they came in contact with. The painted skin colour of the Beothuk Indians of Newfoundland forever gave the name to a race of native people that covered an entire continent."

Howley was silent for a while. "Do you think the Red Indians are still with us, Matthieu?" he asked suddenly.

The fire crackled. Small, black rivulets lapped gently along the beach's edge. The fire glow caught the waves, making them glitter like beaded lace. Behind them, where the beach ended, a great, dark, virgin forest reached into the heavens. Above the trees, glittering stars twinkled and shone. The soft summer night breeze brought to their ears a sighing, gently rushing sound. It was the river that ran unseen into the lake through a deep-wooded canyon off to their left. A pair of loons cried out on the dark lake. Somewhere above them snipes hunted, their trilling cries rising and fading. A mysterious wilderness feeling, an unexplained ancient spirit, had come stealing along.

Howley felt uncomfortable and kept staring into the fire. But Mattie Mitchell looked at the whispering waves that sparkled and shone when they crossed the fire-path and disappeared into blackness after they passed the man-made light. When Mattie spoke, his voice sounded reluctant at first, but soon it resumed the cadence that was his alone. Sitting beside the lake where the Beothuk people had once lived, and with the soft summer spirit listening all around them, Mattie told Howley the Mi'kmaq story of Santu, which had been passed down to him by the elders of his people.

"In time long pas' my people don't come 'ere," he began, indicating with his hand the huge lake that stretched away in the darkness. "Mi'kmaq 'ave saying. Red man's dat way, Mi'kmaq dis way." Mattie pointed in a generally eastern direction for the Beothuk and a westerly one for the Mi'kmaq.

"I nivver see Red Indian. I find ver' many ol' trails not made by Mi'kmaq. One time I find ver' strange wigwam by big river. No one live dere." Mattie stirred the campfire again and appeared to be uneasy.

"Sometime I 'ear soft footfall behind me. No man's dere. Sometime I feel spirit in nighttime. Like dis night. Red man's ghos', maybe." Mattie turned his head and looked all around the black outer rim where the firelight could not reach, as if expecting to see something. Howley knew Mattie was a very spiritual man. He also knew he had a dread of ghosts. It was the only thing that Mattie Mitchell feared.

Mattie spoke again, his voice quieter but steady. "Santu born 'ere by dis water my people call Red Pond," he said. "Santu's mother Mi'kmaq woman. She lie down on beach in summertime wit' Beothuk man. Maybe dis beach!" Mattie looked all around again. "Mi'kmaq woman 'ave girl chil'. Call her Santu. Santu call her father 'Kop.' Dis Mi'kmaq name fer beaver root grow

54

in water. Dis root red like Beothuk man. Mi'kmaq woman, Red Indian man's child 'ave Mi'kmaq blood an' Beothuk blood." He paused in his story and glanced at the sprawling figure of Howley, sensing the man's doubt in the tale. "Santu leave dis place long time ago. She 'ave chil' wit' Beothuk blood." And with that, Mattie rose from the beach and walked past the fire glow. His tall figure disappeared in the dark.

* * * * *

MATTIE MITCHELL AND JAMES HOWLEY left the "Red Pond" the very next morning. They traversed the Victoria and the Lloyd's River systems. Mattie led the way. While Howley sketched his maps and entered the geology of the land, Mattie hunted and fished and provided for them both.

They crossed the rivers and the valleys of this wild land again and again over the next two months. They reached the open caribou barrens of Newfoundland's interior on the south coast, and on a cold, foggy October 27, they stepped tired and hungry onto the white beaches near the fishing outport of Burgeo. Howley's ragged black beard hid most of the sores from the hordes of biting flies, "That forever feasted with great relish on my 'White' blood, yet appeared to dislike the 'Red' blood of my companion."

When they finished the expedition, Howley took away numerous books filled with information about the Newfoundland wilderness that would be used by generations to come. Howley's name would live forever in the many volumes describing his adventures. A town in the forested heart of the island he loved took his name and still bears it today.

But the man who showed him the way across this vast, unknown wilderness, and who hunted and foraged for their camp on this venture, was forgotten.

Years later, American anthropologist Frank Speck would verify Mattie's tale. Speck interviewed an Indian woman in Gloucester, Massachusetts, who told him her father was an Indian from the island of Newfoundland. Her name was Santu. The woman appeared to be approximately seventy-five years of age. This would mean she had been born around 1835. The last known recorded Beothuk was the woman Shanawdithit. She died in 1829.

Santu told Speck her father was a full-blooded Beothuk man from the "Red Pond" of Newfoundland. Santu called the Beothuk Meywe'djidjk, meaning "Red People." Her father's name was "Kop" and her mother was a Mi'kmaq woman. Santu remembered her father very well. She said he squeezed the juice from the red root that grew there and smeared it all over his body, even his loins. They also knew where to find the red earth, which was also used to dye their bodies. The dye would last for half a year.

Santu said her father, Kop, ate meat half-roasted on a stick. He killed caribou with bow and arrows. The arrow that killed the caribou was sacrificed to the animal's spirit and never used again. They travelled to the coast in the springtime, she said, where they hunted *si'kane'su*—whales—using arrows and spears. She remembered being wrapped in a small blanket or *tu* as a child. The woman also told Speck she remembered being bundled in with dogs to keep warm on cold nights.

She still remembered a few words of her father's language. They called rain *gau*. A woman was *be'nam*. When the Beothuk *be'nam* were in their *menses*, they were not permitted to step over a hunter's snowshoes, or even his tracks, for fear of casting a bad spirit upon his hunting. A very fat person was called a *gu'wa*. She even recalled the Beothuk word *se'ko*, which meant "prayer."

The Beothuk were constantly under attack by the white man

from across the sea, according to Santu. Her father, Kop, had been raised by the Mi'kmaq after his people had all been killed by the whites.

Santu had gone to Nova Scotia by canoe. She married a Mohawk Indian and lived in New Brunswick for a while. When her husband died, she married a Mi'kmaq chieftain who was called Toney. Speck interviewed Santu's son, Joe Toney, who told him the same story of the Beothuk man who was his grandfather. His mother had told him the tale over and over again. Joe Toney died in Nova Scotia. He was believed to be 102 years old.

When Howley read the article by Speck, he remembered a warm summer night on Mattie Mitchell's "Red Pond." Most of all he regretted his own doubt in a tale that wasn't properly recorded. He suddenly wondered how many more untold tales Mattie Mitchell had "recorded" in his head.

CHAPTER 5

MATTIE MITCHELL SAW NO OTHER MAN through the long, cold winter. He walked alone over his own snowy, unmarked trails. He established new ones. And always he was the vigilant hunter and consummate trapper. Mattie was as much a part of the land he walked as were the animals he hunted.

His mind held no fear of the trackless wilderness, nor did the long winter night cause him the dread experienced by most of the white men he knew. For him it was simply a dark part of his day, a time for cleaning his furs and mending his garments, a time for silent, much-needed rest.

On blustery days he stayed near his shelter, packing the falling snow again and again around the base and partway up the wall of his wigwam, until the strongest wind could not penetrate it. When the terrible dry cold of the long winter nights set in, the wigwam suddenly turned frigid when the fire died. On such nights, Mattie drank all the water he could hold before "turning in." His swollen bladder always awoke him just in time to add more fuel to the dwindling fire.

To add further insulation against the winter chill, he hung over the inside of his door the partly cured hide of a huge *mui'n*, a black bear. The hide measured longer than Mattie himself.

He had spent hours at night flensing the fat and blood from the big hide. He soaked it in the nearby stream and had allowed the minnows to pick at the last tiny bits of fat until the skin was clean. However, the hide still glistened when the firelight shone on it, turning the tips of the hairs silver.

The hide should fetch a good price on the coast, he figured, although he never knew from one year to the next what money he would receive for his furs. There was one furrier in the Bay of St. George who always gave him a fair price, and although it was far to walk—if he couldn't get a boat ride down the coast with one of the local fishermen, a rare event—Mattie would take his furs nowhere else.

But for now the bear skin would break the draft from his door.

Mattie relished the story of the bear hunt he planned to tell the village children. He seldom talked much with the adults, especially the whites, who for the most part rarely spoke to him at all. But the children were different, Indian as well as white. They always came running to hear his "trapline tales" when he came walking in to the village at the end of each winter. And Mattie never disappointed them.

But it hurt him deeply one evening when a young, blue-eyed white boy with yellow hair, who had been listening with the others, was called home by the relentless shouts of his mother. Mattie heard his angry mother say plainly, her voice carrying on the quiet evening air, "I told you to stay away from dat filthy Injun."

With his usual stoic manner, Mattie bore the taunt, like all of the others he had endured, and said nothing.

* * * * *

THE STORY OF THIS BEAR HUNT HAD begun nearly a year ago, on a late spring morning. The days were getting longer and warmer. The snow was beginning to melt. Geese could be seen flying in wedges against the evening sky, their honking resounding through the hills as they headed north. The nights were getting shorter, but they were still cold enough to freeze the snow.

It was the time of year when a man could walk over the crusted snow without need for snowshoes. It was a time relished by all trappers, since great distances could be covered in a day. It was nearly time to leave the mountains, but Mattie searched early each morning for one more thing. He carried his snowshoes on his back. If he found what he was looking for it would take him far away, and he had no intention of being forced to walk home without them on snow weakened by the sun.

He found exactly what he was looking for on the second morning of his search. Imprinted in the snow's surface were the tracks of a very large black bear. The print that had broken the crust was bigger than Mattie's fully spread hand.

He followed the tracks for just a few minutes. The bear had passed here not long ago. It had been running from tree to tree and paying extra attention to several decayed stumps that it had ripped open. Obviously the bear was very hungry. Mattie had no intention of following the animal at all, though by its spoor he knew it was not a nursing mother, but a male. Its hide was at its worst this time of year and its flesh would be lean and tasteless. The long winter had sapped the animal of its fat reserves. Mattie turned and began back-tracking the bear.

It was easy enough to do. The bear had left a clear but very twisted trail. There wasn't one deadfall or one exposed stump rising up through the snow that the animal hadn't searched thoroughly for food. Mattie figured the bear had come out of its winter den that very morning, and he wanted to find it.

The tracks led him in a general direction toward a high ridge in the distance. He wanted to leave the spoor and cut straight for it, but he couldn't take the chance. Maybe the bear had come from a different direction altogether. He had been fooled before, so now he kept on the tracks. Sometimes they circled and crossed over themselves. He followed them for more than four miles before he knew he was nearing the den.

The spoor led up over an imposing slope that faced south. The warming sun had melted most of the snow away from the place, exposing a wide, talus rubble that had long ago foundered down. Mattie climbed up over the rock slide and was soon standing on a very wide ledge. Over the years, huge boulders had fallen from the hill above, one on top of the other, which he figured had caused the talus slide.

Some of the winter snows had fallen among the boulders, but several feet of them remained visible. This furrow had taken more than its share of drifting snow. It took a while before he found the den opening, so carefully was it hidden. The bear had walked around the site many times before it had finally left the area. Its tracks were everywhere. The smell gave its den site away. It was a heady, musky odour like no other. It wasn't a sharp, tangy, eye-burning scent like castor, or the throat-sticking gland smell from the stag caribou that could sometimes be confused for another animal. This was a strong smell that a man would never forget as being "bear smell."

To get out of its winter home, the bear had pushed aside a mix of boughs and sticks, clumps of moss, and straggly yellow grasses, all of which it had pulled over the opening just before last winter's big snowfall. The "doorway" was big enough for Mattie to squeeze through on his belly, but the debris the bear had piled up in front of the den allowed very little light in, and Mattie wriggled back out without getting a good look inside.

Standing up, he studied the way he had come while following

the bear's tracks. He would not be returning to his camp the same way.

Walking down over the rock avalanche, he stopped and looked around. He would come back in late autumn to hunt the bear. He knew that if he came back here again and there was little or no snow at all, the place would look much different. Turning his head slowly, he took in every detail of the place. And then he walked back to his wigwam.

In the early days of the next trapping season, Mattie set out for the bear den. The sky looked like a storm was brewing. He hoped he had timed it right. The going was much harder than it had been in the spring. He walked in a straight line as much as the terrain allowed. Twice he had to veer away from his course to get around small ponds that had not frozen solidly enough for safe travel. By late evening he reached the talus slope below the cave where the bear had sheltered from the freezing cold of the winter past.

Mattie wondered if his long walk had been in vain. Maybe the bear had not returned here this year. If it had, it would be days before the animal decided to enter the den. But a heavy snowstorm this time of year would decide for the bear, and the sky looked ready to snow. Mattie had seen the big bears foraging for food even in mid-January. However, when a big snow came and made food hard to find, even this early in the season, they always "denned up."

Mattie was prepared to wait. He wanted to catch the bear near its den. During his walk he had crushed the green needles of the white spruce into his hands and smeared their pungent scent all over his clothing several times. It was his proven method of approaching game undetected.

He would have to be extremely wary. Black bears had poor eyesight, but their sense of hearing and their incredible sense of smell more than compensated for that. They could detect and identify the wind-borne scent of food miles away. They especially hated the smell of humans, and when they sensed it they made every effort to avoid its source.

The full carcass of an adult black bear would keep Mattie in fat for frying and tallow for light, and proved a ready supply of delicious meat for most of the winter. The animal's fur, which would now be at its prime, was another bonus. For now, though, Mattie wanted bear meat. He loved the taste of it.

Mattie knew the bear would disappear inside its den for the winter after the first big snow. He knew of white trappers who shot the bears, males and nursing females alike, while they slept inside their caves. But Mattie Mitchell always called it the coward's way of hunting, and he was no coward.

He decided not to climb the scree slope. To do so quietly would be difficult, and if the bear was in the area, an unusual sound would alert it and make it that much more vigilant. Mattie knew no one had been here since he had left several months ago. He hoped the bear was feeling safe and, with a full belly, lethargic.

Downwind and off to the side of the talus was a thick copse which he hoped would conceal him on his way up to the ledge. When he approached it he found it did indeed provide some cover. This was a much easier way up over the ridge.

But the bear had thought so, too. Twisting its way through the gnarled brush and tangled trees was its well-used trail. It wasn't easy going for a man of Mattie's height. The bear, walking on all fours, had fashioned a trail fairly close to the ground. Besides, Mattie considered, he would surely leave his man scent, no matter how hard he tried to disguise it. He decided to abandon this course of action.

It was hard, slow going, but he stealthily made his way up

through the ravine, parallel to the bear lead. The low scrub spruce and thorny bushes struggled for growth beneath short, twisted, naked yellow birches. Here in the relative shelter of the cliff there was no more than a skim of snow.

The floor of the steep ravine was strewn with rocks of all sizes, with only a sparse layer of wet, clinging soil. This was a snarly, tangled place to get through quietly, but he finally reached the edge of the boulder train above, where no trees grew.

At first he thought he had been mistaken as he peered carefully out of his cover. When he had been here last there had been at least seven feet of snow on the ground. The place looked different now, as he knew it would. But then he smelled the heady bear odour, and with his nose directing him, he saw the den's opening.

The hole between the tumbled grey boulders looked bigger than it had in the winter. The bear had dragged a pile of debris and spread it all around the entry. Birch trees the thickness of Mattie's forearm had been broken and chewed off and dragged to the site. Green fir saplings, as well as fir boughs torn from low-hanging trees, last year's dried boughs with brown needles clinging to them weakly, clumps of yellow-green moss and fallen leaves, mud, and a few rocks littered the area. All was in readiness for the bear to crawl inside, pull the debris over the opening, and rest up for the coming winter.

This was a cleverly chosen place for the animal to hibernate. The small space between the opening and the gathered refuse was angled toward the den. The beast would merely have to reach out, and with one easy pull, the debris would tumble toward the "doorway." The falling snow would not only disguise its winter resting place, but seal the bear from the outside world for months.

All of this Mattie could see from his hidden vantage point. He had seen many such places before, but he had never witnessed such a large pile or such large items comprising such a collection before. This was no ordinary bear! He was sure of it.

He had not been too late. He was right about that. The bear had not yet crawled into its den.

But Mattie would find out that he was wrong about that.

All was quiet, save for the swish of wind searching through the green trees and the rustle of leaves fluttering down through bare branches. Somewhere in the valley below him a raven croaked a few times and then was silent. Then the wind suddenly breezed up and it started to snow.

He checked his old Martin Henry rifle. It was loaded with one long, brass-coated bullet. He considered pulling the hammer to full cock. This bear would not give him much time. Still, the old rifle had seen better days. The cock-spring had weakened over the years and, when fully cocked, could not be depended on to "stand cock." He pulled the hammer to "half dog," put an extra bullet in the palm of his left hand, and, holding the big gun in his right hand, settled down to wait.

The evening wore on and still the bear did not show. The wind increased out of the northeast, the noise of its steady brewing now a constant torment. The snow started to accumulate. Mattie suddenly realized that he had made a big mistake in his hurry to get here. He had forgotten to bring his snowshoes! If this was going to be a major winter storm, the walk back to his camp would not be any easy one. But, in his usual calm way, he resigned himself to the task at hand.

Mattie kept looking at the entrance and the bear trail, only a few feet from where he waited downwind. He expected the bear to come ambling along at any moment. The falling snow was the wet, plastering kind. He was getting cold and he wanted to stand and warm himself. But for now he dared not move.

When the dark time was near, he decided to stand. Heavy

snow was falling. The snowflakes came tumbling out of the sky like swarms of white moths. Mattie would leave and find a place to spend the night and return in the morning. If he discovered the bear had entered the den during the night, he would rouse it out and shoot it. It was a simple enough plan.

He stepped quietly from his cover and brushed away some of the snow from his clothing. His shoulders and knees were getting wet. His step was soundless in the wet snow, and walking over to the hoard of debris, he crept over it and bent over, peering down into the cave. Like the last time he had been here, he couldn't see much of anything.

His curiosity got the better of him. Laying down his gun and facing the cave entrance, he wormed his long body inside. The musky bear smell was almost overpowering. But another of his senses warned him too late—the unmistakable feeling of sudden warmth. The bear was inside! And following that realization, into Mattie's view came a wide, brown, snuffling nose cradled between a set of long and sharp, dirty-white claws.

The bear spat a deep, gruff warning from between its teeth as it coughed Mattie's hated man-smell out of its sensitive, flaring nostrils. The whites of its eyes rolled in disbelief at what it saw. Mattie knew he was in deep trouble. He squirmed backwards like a crab caught on a hot beach at low tide. His coat caught and rolled up over his back. His hat came off.

He pushed clear of the narrow opening and thrust himself to a standing position, gun in hand, when the bear came roaring out of the hole and lunged at him. From waist high Mattie pointed the gun at the black mass and pulled the trigger.

His finger stalled on the cold, unresisting steel. Mattie realized in disbelief that the gun was not at full cock. He hauled the hammer all the way back and heard the distinctive click as the hammer went into "full dog." The huge bear was directly above him.

Mattie stumbled backwards over the heap. Mid-fall, he pointed the muzzle up at the heaving animal's chest and yanked the trigger again. The rifle roared out its bullet. The bear's dense, black hide muffled the report. It dropped, spread-eagled, upon Mattie, and its clawed feet scrambled for purchase.

Its front paws were on the ground just beyond Mattie's shoulders, but its hind feet had landed fully upon his upper thighs. For what seemed like an eternity, the bear's undersides mashed against his face. The stench of its hide filled his nose and the long, stiff hair filled his mouth. He couldn't breathe. Then there came a terrible pressure against his right thigh as the animal scrambled once again for footing. For a second he thought he was free . . . but then the bear fell again.

The animal's heavy, swaying hindquarters barely cleared Mattie's head. When it collapsed again its two back claws lay in twitching spasms on each of Mattie's shoulders. He felt a hot liquid spray over his left shoulder and thought it was blood. However, it smelled acrid and musky. The bear's bladder muscles had let go.

Mattie twisted away from the weight of the beat's hindquarters and got on his knees. He pulled the long, empty casing out of the gun. Realizing he had lost the bullet he had been holding, he fumbled in his pants pocket for the only one he had left. Then he realized the bear was not moving. It was dead.

The wind howled down the hills. Mattie staggered back and sat on the pile of refuse the bear had gathered to cover its den. A shudder of fear washed over him. It was the first time he had experienced such a feeling. He had played a part in many dangerous situations in the wilderness, but none of them had brought him as close to dying as this one. It suddenly came to him that his stumbling over the pile had saved his life. The mess of sticks and earth had broken the bear's first terrible lunge.

And as suddenly as the fearful feeling had come, it left him and he was his old practical, thinking self again. Then he felt a trickle of blood running down his right leg. The bear had torn what felt like several long, deep gashes into the upper muscle of his thigh. He felt a burning sensation that quickly graduated to a painful throb. Mattie took a careful look at the bear to make sure it was dead. Its hairy black hide was turning white with snow.

Mattie was wet and cold. He had a bad wound that needed attention and no shelter from the night blizzard that was upon him. And then he thought of the warm, dry bear den.

The bear was a very large male, or what Mattie called "The Dog." There would be no other bears coming close to its den. And so, with the common sense and simple at-hand solutions that were his trademark, Mattie Mitchell slowly squirmed his way into the hole in the rocks that the bear had so quickly vacated.

Once inside the initial opening he discovered the place was fairly large, or at least what he could see of it in the murky darkness. He reached all around and above his head and judged the cave to be several feet wide and close to five feet high, and while he would not be able to stand, he could sit up comfortably.

His first need was a fire. His leg caused him a great deal of pain after the bleeding had slowed to a trickle. He crawled back to the opening and began tearing at the debris. It was surprisingly easy.

Digging through it, he found plenty of seasoned wood. There were dozens of pieces of birch bark, the best of fire starters. This place had obviously been occupied by bears for a long time. The pile of wood and earth was much deeper than it had appeared. Despite the high wind and falling snow, it only took him a few minutes to get a fire started at the cave entrance, and before long the flames flickered inside, serving to warm and cheer him up.

The tear in his pant leg was small and would be easily mended, but his leg would need much attention. By the scant light of the fire he inspected the wound. He was surprised to see that his skin had been punctured in only two places. One of the cuts was much deeper and longer than the other.

Ignoring the searing pain that was increasing by the minute, he made his way back to the opening. By the light of the fire, he broke off several branches of the young fir trees the bear had hauled near to its dwelling place. Back inside, he cut the branches into manageable pieces. He was pleased to see the tree had many small myrrh bladders on it. Holding them over his wounds, he drained the sticky contents of a few of the bladders directly into both of the cuts. He winced a bit when the cold myrrh contacted his open wounds, but he smeared the sticky substance all over them anyway.

Peeling several strips from the tree branches, he wound their white, silky-smooth inner bark—with the smooth side against his wounds—around his leg, covering the cuts completely. He tucked the strip ends, one beneath the other, without using a knot. He wished he had more myrrh, but for now it would have to do.

Looking around his shelter, he could see that it was not as spacious as he had at first assumed, but it would suit his purpose just fine. It was amazingly clean. He was fairly warm. He had gotten used to the bear smell. A nest of grass and bark at the end farthest from the opening was where the bear had prepared its bed. It took up most of the entire back end of the cave. Mattie had not gotten a good look at the animal, but he knew for certain this was no ordinary bear.

That night, and for two more nights, Mattie Mitchell stayed near the dead bear's lair. For two of those days it snowed without letting up. He managed to gut and skin the bear, and when he laid the rich black hide out on the snow, he looked at it in disbelief. He lay down beside it and discovered it was much taller than he.

Mattie nursed his wound and feasted. He ate the heart and liver and kidneys of the bear first. He cut prime strips from high on its back bone and roasted them over his fire.

In the clear, cold dawn of the fourth day, he made his way back to his camp. It was a laborious trip for him, due as much to travelling over the deep snow without snowshoes as to his injured thigh. But just as night slid down from the hills, Mattie Mitchell walked into his wigwam with dark on his shoulder.

It took him two more trips with his komatik to get the bear carcass and the heavy hide home. The torn flesh in his thigh healed perfectly, but the scars from the biggest bear he had ever hunted remained with him for the rest of his life.

* * * * *

MATTIE TOLD THE STORY OF HIS GREATEST bear hunt to enthusiastic children in his village many times. But the story was never told with so much passion as it was by another man, many years after the old woodsman had died.

This man sat in a creaking rocking chair in the warmth of his kitchen. Sitting across from him, his young son listened spellbound. The boy strained to hear every last word. When the father had finished the story, he looked into the blue eyes of his only son and suddenly realized something.

When Mattie Mitchell had told that story so long ago, the white boy had sneaked up behind the fence, unbeknownst to his stern mother, and, with his ear close to the rotting pickets, had heard every word the hunter had said.

What he had just realized as he looked at the intent face of his son was, on that evening so long ago, he did not have to strain to hear Mattie's story. Mattie had talked loudly that evening. It was just not something the Indian did. Mattie Mitchell had known the white boy was listening and had spoken loud enough for him to hear.

The man, whose yellow hair was now grey, reached out and, placing his hand on the boy's shoulder, said, "I hope you will always see the true colour of a man, my son. Time for bed now."

And then the boy ran across the floor, his yellow hair bouncing. Turning at the foot of the stairs, he said, "Good night, Pop," and the man in the suddenly silent rocking chair said, "Good night, Matthew."

CHAPTER 6

MATTIE WAS A MAN OF MANY TALES. He especially loved telling his wilderness stories to children, white or native. They were always a willing audience who never interrupted. He seldom told his stories to the elders of his own people, and never to the adult white people.

There was one story, though, which he told to no one but the Mi'kmaq children. Whenever he told it, he always told it in the only language in which it had been told to him, the ancient Mi'kmaq. He always started the tale by telling the youngsters how and where he had heard the story.

He was only a boy then, he said, and the only child his parents ever had. His father was still alive but very sick. When the children learned that Mattie had been a boy himself when he had first heard the tale, they gathered around his feet. They seemed to be listening with their eyes, which stared at the hunter without blinking, as if by doing so they would miss something.

"My father ver' sick man. He cough ver' much," he said. "Ol' ones come with ver' much medicine for 'im. Dey sit long time in wigwam. Dey tell many yarns. But dis yarn dey tell only in nighttime 'round campfire. Dey never tell to white man. White man never believe dis story." Mattie looked all around as if checking to see if there were any white adults present before continuing.

It was a story about a Beothuk hunter and warrior. Bukashaman was a young Beothuk Indian from the "Red Pond." The Mi'kmaq called him Buka.

Buka had lain with a very pretty woman of his own tribe. She was called Tehobosheen or Tehonee. The couple had a girl child they named Kuisduit. Tehonee called their daughter Kuise, but Buka always called his pretty daughter Small One. She never lived long enough to be called anything else. Both little Kuise and her mother, Tehonee, were killed on a beach by the white man's guns. Their cruel deaths changed Buka from a peaceful hunter to a fierce, vengeful warrior.

Mattie remembered where he had heard the tale first. It was on the sandy shores deep in the bay the white men called Halls Bay. The wigwam they lived in had only recently been built above the beach at the edge of the forest. His father had moved with his family as far away from the few white settlers as he could get when the sickness came. It was the white man's disease, he said.

It was summertime, the time of gathering riches from the blue sea. His father planned to move farther inland when the leaves turned. He did not make it, Mattie said, but died in a bout of coughing a few days later.

His father's cough had been strangely silent during this story's telling, Mattie said. The old man who told the tale stood in their wigwam and with much shadowed gesticulations told the tale that had been heard and told again and again, passed on beside countless campfires. He began by describing in great detail what happened when Buka saw his very first white man.

* * * * *

FROM THE CORNER OF THE DENSE WOODS, Buka stared at the strange men. Most of them had ugly hair on their faces and from here he could smell their terrible odour. Their heads were covered with a black, shapeless garment that hung over their ears and partially covered their hair. This tangled mess that grew to their shoulders and covered some of their faces was of different colours and not at all like the red men.

One stranger's hair was the colour of dead grass, while another's was almost the deep red of the ochre that Buka wore on his skin. He stared at this one the longest, wondering where he had found the precious dye, and why he would shade his unruly hair with it. The redheaded man also had blotches of the red mud on his otherwise white face, as if he had run out of the dye before he could completely cover his face, which, unlike the other men, was hairless.

Their huge *tapoteek* were drawn close to the rough shore and were fastened with long, braided strands the likes of which he had never seen. The boats themselves were not made of bark, but of wood. This he could determine from his vantage point. The newcomers were full of mystery and carried themselves with an arrogant and carefree demeanour. They were living on the Beothuk land without permission and yet posted no guard, nor, from what Buka could see, showed any concern for their surroundings.

One man stood apart from the others. He was beardless and carried himself differently. His eyes scanned the woods in a searching stare and, once, his gaze fell across the low clump of trees where the red man lay hidden. But the white man didn't see anything and soon returned to the noisy group. Buka stared long and hard at this tall, lean man and decided that he must be their chief.

The red hunter crept closer to a better vantage point. Holding still and motionless, he watched and waited. Presently, one of the heavily clothed men emerged from the nearby log structure. The solid wood opening that he stepped through squealed at his appearance and complained even louder when he closed the door behind him. This man was almost as tall as the observant one and, although he wore a long, grey, grizzled beard, he resembled the other clean-shaven one in his long stride and commanding attitude.

At a rough command from this man, one of the other men walked briskly to the shoreline and stepped lively out over a short, log-built wharf where the big boat bobbed on its painter. Leaning against the rope, he pulled the vessel closer to the crude dock and jumped aboard. Buka was amazed to see the boat barely move at such an indignity, a motion that would have sunk and probably destroyed his own *tapoteek*.

The white man bent below the gunnels of the boat and soon stood erect again, holding a large fish in each hand. He threw both fish onto the deck of the wharf. Again and again he repeated the work, now using a long handle with a sharp, curved end, pronging the fish in their white stomachs. He sometimes flung two and three at once upon the narrow log surface. As the hunter watched, his mouth watered for the delicious codfish that lay on the wharf before him. Never had he seen so many *bobusowet* at one time.

Soon the boat was emptied and the fisherman joined the others on the shore. Now the work of cleaning the catch began in earnest. There was a short, rectangular table set up, made of small, round logs. Onto this the fat fish were placed one by one. Using a long, shiny knife, one of the men eviscerated the large *bobusowet*. He pulled the twin white livers from the dead fish and threw them into a puncheon nearby. The stench of the livers fermenting in the huge barrel stirred anew with each addition.

Another, shorter man, his face hidden by a tangle of dried, grass-coloured hair, seized the gutted cod and placed his left hand on the open breast of the fish, his right hand holding its head below the sharpened edge of the table. With one of his thumbs and one of his fingers poked into the eye sockets of the fish, he gave a quick, violent push, one hand against the other, and removed the head before throwing it back in the water. Here the raucous seagulls swooped and dipped and fought over the offal, their cries filling the narrow cove.

The tall, clean-faced man was next to grasp the fish. Using a shorter, slightly curved knife, he removed the long backbone in three clean sweeps of his blade. The red man's curiosity knew no bounds. More than anything, the Beothuk was fascinated with the knives and their unbelievable sharpness. He leaned so far out of his hiding place to better see the wondrous knives that, if the strangers had been watching, he would have been seen.

For more than two hours he watched these strange men with the pale skin clean the huge catch of fish. When they had finished and had thrown all the entrails into the sea at their feet, they removed the fish, glistening with sea water, from the great round, wooden, water-filled vat.

As he watched, the men carried layers of the split cod into a three-walled lean-to nearby. From his position he could see inside this crude structure, which was close to his hiding place. Placing the fish on the lungered floor, one of the men brought forth, from a small barrel inside, buckets of a white, granular substance which he proceeded to fling over the bodies of the spread cod without cease until they were completely covered.

Their rough voices came to him easily, some of them high-pitched and squeaky and others deep and growly. Not at all like the language of the true people.

Why would men in heavy, smelly clothes do such a thing?

To catch and carefully clean more cod than he had ever seen in one place, only to cover them with a coarse white sand? The cod his people managed to catch they hung over the smoke fires and cured to a delicious taste that always gave them energy and full bellies. Looking at the gulls screaming and feeding on the guts of the fish, Buka's mouth watered for all the sweet-tasting hearts the white men had so carelessly discarded. They were a delicacy and were best eaten raw, fresh out of the still-wriggling fish.

To further amaze the Indian, the noisy men strode away from their fish-cleaning place and left their shiny knives stuck in the wooden table. He couldn't believe that such treasures would be left unguarded. His own knife never left his side and he was always conscious of it. His very survival depended on it.

The night crept in over the grey sea in ever-deepening shadows on the still bay, until the land across the quite cove was black, with only a faint glow from the dying day left on the water. Soon, that last vestige of the light that had been, was gone and the cove was filled with night. Small, sighing waves touched and whispered around the rocks.

The stars appeared as if by magic, until the sky was filled with their wonder, and still Buka waited. The noise inside the log dwelling finally quieted. Countless moths and mosquitoes flew toward a small light inside, which had dimmed until it gave no useful light at all. Heavy snores followed out through the chinks of the poorly built shack where the invaders slept.

Leaving his cramped hiding place, he ran silently along the beach near the water's edge. He stayed crouched over in a quiet jog until he arrived at the foul-smelling wharf. Stopping and listening, he watched the effervescent remains of the cod entrails swaying back and forth with the silent tide. Small splashes broke the water surface as hidden night fishes closed in on the offal. His muscles had relaxed with the short sprint along the beach, and now he sprang up onto the surface of the log wharf in as graceful and fluid a motion as that of a lynx.

Bent over, he remained motionless, waiting for signs of discovery. There were none, only the small lops against the rickety pier beneath his feet and a few muffled snores in the distance. Two steps more and still bent over, he was beside the small table. Pieces of cod guts hung over the edge and dark blotches of blood stained its surface. It smelled terrible.

He reached up over the table's edge and with both hands pulled the two shiny knives from the sodden, musty wood. He couldn't believe it had been so easy. The feel of the knives in his hand fascinated him. He instinctively knew their worth. Holding them by their smooth, wooden handles, he crept in over the shaky, lungered wharf until he was once again on the land and closer to the sleeping strangers.

The smell of the stacked fish in the small shelter drew him. He paused and forced himself to listen once again. The night was still. The sleeping white men inside the big log mamateek were oblivious to their stealthy night visitor.

Reaching the tier of stacked *bobusowet*, he almost retched at the strong smell. But his curiosity prevailed and, reaching down, Buka grabbed one of the fish by the tail and pulled it free from its salty bed.

Back along the shingled beach, he ran, both knives in his right hand and the white-coated cod dripping in his left. When he had cleared the beach and had gone for several minutes more into the shrouded forest, he stopped to inspect his good fortune.

The knives he tossed from hand to hand, their balance and the feel of them a pure joy to his hunter's soul. He tested them against the tree bark, peeling the rough spruce bark effortlessly. He could only imagine the ease with which he could clean an animal with such a tool, although the curved knife puzzled him.

Maybe it was only used to cut the big bone from the *bobusowet*, a practice he had never seen before. Very pleased with his find, he didn't consider stealing them wrong. The knives had been left unguarded. He had simply taken them. He would fully expect the same done to him, if he were foolish enough to leave such valuables unattended.

Buka now turned his attention to the pungent codfish. Peering at it in the darkness, he tore a strip from its thick breast and pushed a piece of it into his mouth. For a second he was puzzled, then revolted, as an unexpected taste exploded in his mouth. Spewing the fish out of his mouth, he retched again and again, trying to rid his mouth of the putrid taste. Reaching to the ground he pulled several leaves from the bushes. He crushed them in his hands, stuffed the leaves into his mouth, and chewed them into a pulp before spitting the entire contents away, sluicing most of the foul-tasting fish with it. He flung the fish away into the night, where it fell with a soft thud among the bushes.

What manner of creatures were these men with the white skin, who would catch so many of the sweet-tasting *bobusowet* only to spoil them all with their cruel-tasting sand? Several times he hawked the salty bile out of his throat, and still the bittersweet salt residue remained, assailing his sensitive taste buds.

Only when he had recovered from the shock of the experience, and had rinsed and cleansed his mouth several times by drinking from a small stream, did he recognize the taste that had invaded his mouth. It was the taste of sea water, only many times greater. But why the strangers had used it on the fish, or where it had come from, mystified him.

Leaving the wooded shoreline behind and climbing the slope in the darkness, he was soon away from the coast and the threat of being discovered. He crawled underneath the overhanging branches of a huge she-spruce and, squirming around a few times, soon fashioned a rough bed for himself on the hard ground. He spat the last of the tainted fish taste out of his mouth, surprised that the sensation still remained. And without a thought to any further comfort, and smiling at the feel of the new knives he had taken, he lay down upon the earth and went instantly to sleep.

* * * * *

SILENCE GREETED MATTIE WHEN he finished his tale. The children stared at him in wonder, their mouths agape. They all wanted to hear more about Buka the Red Indian warrior. But Mattie told them, "You mus' listen ver' many times to one story. When you kin tell it same way to someone else, den you ready to 'ear more 'bout Buka the true Red Indian."

"Mattie came down out of the hills
bringing dark on his shoulder."

ILLUSTRATION BY CLINT COLLINS

CHAPTER 7

ELWOOD WORCESTER WAS BORN IN Massillon, Ohio, on May 16, 1862. As a young man working in a dingy, cramped railway office after the death of his father left his family in poverty, he had what for him was a life-changing experience. One day his dark office was suddenly filled with a brilliant unnatural light. From somewhere beyond the steady, surreal gleam of light, a strong but very clear, soft voice said, "Be faithful to me and I will be faithful to you."

After that he became an ordained Episcopalian minister. He was the founder of the Emmanuel Movement of America, whose philosophy attributed physical, mental, and nervous problems as well as psychotherapy with the spiritual well-being of the human mind. Worcester founded the Boston Society for Psychic Research. His activities played a major role in helping with research for the dreaded disease tuberculosis.

But Worcester was something more. He was an avid sportsman. He went to great lengths and took advantage of every opportunity to experience the wonders of hunting and fishing all over North America. He regarded it as "one of my choice blessings that these pleasures have never palled on me." The preacher would think nothing of walking the great distance along a terrible trail to Irondequoit Bay, in Lake Ontario, just to fish for a few yellow perch, several black bass, or even sunfish.

Having heard about the wonders of northern Canada and the largely unexplored regions of that vast country, he decided to go there. Worcester obtained rail passage to Quebec, where he arranged for four native Indians, who spoke no English and knew only a few words of the French language, to take him into the interior.

They left Lac-Saint-Jean, headwaters of the mighty Saguenay River, and made their laborious way north by canoe into the lonely, uninhabited wilderness of Quebec. Weeks later and several hundred miles away from any human habitation, Worcester had finally experienced enough of the north wilds. Blaming the whole unpleasant ordeal on his "four ignorant Indian guides," he returned to the modern world vowing never to use Indians as guides again. Then he met Mattie Mitchell.

* * * * *

ANOTHER OF WORCESTER'S PASSIONS was reading, when he could find the time. He especially loved browsing through historical accounts about Canada, partly because of its self-proclaimed status as a sportsman's paradise, and partly due to his recent disappointing foray into that north land.

What he found one day, while reading a historical work in the city of Philadelphia, was a riveting account of another northern country—Newfoundland. He relished the writings of John and Sebastian Cabot. The descriptions the two men had given about their "discovery" of the island of Newfoundland fascinated him. The Cabots had found scores of fishes "great and small." Vast shoals of cod were taken from the virgin blue sea as easily as dipping them up with a simple basket. Silvery salmon and gleaming trout they scooped from the shallow rivers. They salted down barrels of the protein-rich fish.

Foraging upon the unspoiled land, Cabot's men with their long-barrelled muskets brought back the carcasses of tender caribou and excited tales of "numberless fleet footed Deeres." Their flesh too was salted for transport across the ocean. Animal skins for a fur-hungry England were stowed aboard their ships. All of these trophies, which were taken back to England, served as mere samples of what this "New World" had to offer to the explorers.

But of all the amazing events the Cabots had recounted, one of them stuck in Worcester's mind above all of the rest. The man the English called John Cabot—whose birth name, Giovanni Caboto, was Italian, and whose only known signature appears as Zuan Chabotto—gave to Henry VII, the Tudor king of England, three wondrous pearls. The three pearls had been taken from the shells of freshwater mollusks pulled from just one of the countless rivers of that far-off "New Founde Land."

This revelation, so boldly recorded by these European adventurers hundreds of years ago, played upon the good reverend's mind. He was awakened in the middle of one winter's night by a dream about pearls. He sat upright in his warm featherbed, and there and then decided to plan a trip north to Newfoundland the very next spring. As an added bonus, this big island was the only place left in the world where one could fly-fish Atlantic salmon freely.

Tales of caribou with antler points by the dozens, huge, shiny black bears unequalled anywhere could be hunted there. Worcester couldn't wait for the winter to pass. This time, though, he would not allow Indians to guide him, if there were any on that island in the sea.

Worcester arrived on Newfoundland's coal-burning ferry boat

in early June and decided he would need a sturdy schooner for his coastal explorations of the river mouths. In the rugged outport town of Port aux Basques, where the ferry docked, he was told there wasn't a schooner for sale. However, one of the fishermen knew of a "right smart scunner fer sale in Bay of Islands," a deep fjord farther north along the island's west coast.

It took him several days of walking and hitching boat rides with the friendly fishermen before he arrived in the Bay of Islands. Worcester was enchanted by the rawness of the place. It seemed like the entrance to every cove gave a more spectacular vista than the one before it: massive fjords, their many valleys and gorges filled with the lush green of virgin forests; waterfalls that fell from great heights, with silvery mists marking their fall below the treed skyline; high, flat-topped mountains came down to the sea edge; green canyons twisting around the mountain bases beckoned a man into their realms.

And all of it largely unexplored.

The young, ruddy-faced fisherman back in Port aux Basques who had told him about the schooner had not lied. The vessel was still available. Its owner was now unable to fish for a living.

Frank was a man in his mid-fifties, but his weathered face made him look much older. The man frequently coughed, and walked with a knotty wooden cane. Both men walked out over a large wharf to which the schooner was securely tied fore and aft with heavy manila lines.

A bright, hand-painted board with the name *Danny Boy* was attached to the vessel's stern below her low taffrail. The tide was out, and Worcester knew the schooner was his as soon as he looked down on her neat, spotless single deck, with small double doors in her forecastle swung wide to allow the warm sun into the dark cabin.

Without climbing aboard, although the schooner's owner had

invited him to do just that, Worcester wanted to know the asking price. The man leaned heavily on the cane cut by his own hand, started to speak, and went into a spasm of coughing. He quickly recovered, spat a grey ball of phlegm down into the harbour water, and answered this way:

"I cut every stick out of the hills behind ye. Me boy was still in school then, but he helped with what he could, I will give him dat. Danny, his name is, but we all the time calls him Danny B'y. So we called the scunner after our b'y." His voice seemed to weaken a bit at the mention of his son. Then he continued.

"Mucked the logs and crooked timbers fer her frame on me back and hand slide alike, in its turn. Chopped the timbers meself, I did, and nailed every plank from garbit to gunnel, rammed her tight as a drum wit' oakum I spun wid me own two hands. 'Er decks are poured with heavy pitch too, dey is—not that cheap, runny tar that sticks to a man's rubbers on hot days and always laiks."

Here Frank turned away and coughed again before continuing. Worcester was fascinated with the man's language. His rapid conversation was aided with arm and hand gestures just as quick. He pointed toward the forested hills, the long blue bay, the harbour, or the newly painted schooner as his talk warranted.

Frank's chest-heaving cough produced another pearl-grey issue that he again spat over the wharf edge. Worcester thought he noticed flecks of blood mixed with the sputum as the man cleared his throat and continued his conversation as though he had not stopped.

"I wuz askin' $1,900 fer 'er, sir, but she was just launched fer dis year's fishin' and she'll laik a wee bit at first. 'Twill tek a few days fer 'er seams to plim up. She'll laik nar drop after dat. So I'm askin' $1,850, to 'low fer dat inconvenience every spring to the man wot buys 'er. I won't change me mind on that price, though, sir. Dat's me final one. An' I feels right sure I won't be gyppin' a man wit' it."

Worcester smiled at the man's honesty—when he finally figured out what he had said. When Frank explained what "plim" meant, he willingly agreed to the price.

"Cash on the barrelhead," cautioned the wily old fisherman. When Worcester asked if there were any papers to sign, he replied, "A man's 'and on it is good nuff fer me, sir." Spitting into his right palm, he offered it to the American, who very reluctantly shook it—remembering the spitting—sealing the deal.

Worcester was now the proud owner of a handcrafted, thirty-nine-foot, seaworthy schooner. She was supposed to be forty feet long, Frank told him, but, "Da stem piece I cut 'ad a bit too much rake to it fer me likin', so I shartened 'er keel a bit."

Worcester decided not to ask what it all meant. Counting out the American bills, he told a beaming Frank he loved the boat just as she was and that he would move his gear aboard the *Danny Boy* immediately.

While Frank counted out the most money he had ever held in his hand—after being assured the odd-looking bills were not only good but worth more than the island's currency, something he did not understand—Worcester asked him where he could obtain the services of a good local guide. He wanted someone who not only knew about hunting but also someone who knew the rivers well. Worcester never brought up his intention to search for freshwater clams.

Frank looked up from his money and replied without hesitation. "Mattie Mitchell is the man fer you, sir. He is an Injun man but as good as ar white man, better dan some of da ones I knows about."

Remembering his experience with the Quebec Indians, Worcester replied, "There must be a few white hunters and trappers around these parts that could show me around this country. I will need such a man for a few weeks and I will pay him, of course."

"Dere are some as you say, sir, right smart hunters and good at trappin', too, fer dat matter. But Mattie is still your man, sir." And again gesticulating with his skinny arms, he went on. "I does some huntin' and a bit of trappin' too in the fall time. Dat's after me voyage of fish 'as been made and shipped away, ya know. An' I knows the hills pretty good meself." Here Frank threw his arms wide, indicating the surrounding green mountains.

"But Mattie, sir, is a long cut above me er anyone else dat I knows of in dat regard. Dis man knows the country like the back of 'is own 'and an' farther away dan dat. You won't find no one close to 'e's equals anywhere on dis coast, er any other one on dis island, sir. I knows him well, sir. Jes' dis marnin' he paddled along be me wharf in dat old canoe of 'is, on his way out the bay. Won't be gone more dan two days, I figure. Didn't have no gear aboard dat I could see. Don't talk much, Mattie don't—not like me, eh?" Here Frank smiled, showing strong, tobacco-stained teeth.

For the next two days, Worcester explored the village. He met almost all of the friendly men, a few of the women, and several of the children who followed the 'Merican man around.

* * * * *

ON THE THIRD EVENING, WITH THE SUN down behind the flat mountains and the gloaming casting long shadows out over the still fjord, Mattie Mitchell came paddling toward the schooner where Worcester stood waiting. The Indian was dipping his paddle into the water on the left side of the shallow canoe. Even at a distance, Worcester, who knew about canoes, could see the man was using the J-stroke, a method of paddling that at the end of each long stroke curved outward, which kept the craft straight without having to change sides.

The single paddle flashed and sparkled each time it drew quietly out of the black water. Just as quietly, it plunged back down to the full extent of the Indian's powerful reach. The curved bow of the canoe pushed little bubbles ahead of itself as it came merrily along. The bubbles suddenly fell away from the small craft when Worcester called to the Indian, "Are you Mattie Mitchell, sir?"

"Yes," came the simple reply from the straight-backed man sitting in the stern of the slowing craft.

"May I have a moment of your time, sir?" Worcester asked, hoping the man would paddle closer. The Indian neither moved nor answered for a moment. He and the canoe sat silhouetted like a painting in the still evening water.

One long pull of his paddle brought Mattie Mitchell within a few feet of the black schooner's starboard side, where he stopped and looked up at the man whom he knew to be an American.

"You buy Frank's *Danny B'y* schooner, maybe." He made it sound like he already knew the answer.

"Indeed I have. I have made it my home these last few days. I am quite pleased with the purchase, though I have not sailed her yet," replied Worcester.

"She plim up good yet?"

Pleased that he now understood the word, Worcester smiled down at the Indian. "Yes, the vessel has plimmed very well. I have pumped her only once in three days and that only took a few moments to do," he said, pointing to the homemade wooden pump on the schooner's deck.

Worcester decided this Indian was different than the ones he had encountered in Quebec. He changed the subject toward his reason for being here. "Frank tells me that you are an excellent hunter and trapper as well as a very knowledgeable person regarding the country around these parts."

The canoe bobbed closer to the schooner. Mattie put his left hand against its sleek sides. Looking up, he said, "Frank is good man, fer a white feller. He cough too much, I t'ink. His Millie good woman, too. She bake best bread loaf."

"Indeed she does. I have never tasted better. As a matter of fact, I have a loaf of Millie's excellent bread aboard. The kettle is ready. Would you like a cup of tea?" Worcester asked, noting the concern for Frank evident in Mattie's voice. He decided to stay away from that topic for now.

"You have sugar?" asked a hopeful Mattie, who was moving toward the wharf.

"A big jar of it sitting on the table below, as well as a full bag stored away in the hold. And you are welcome to as much of it as you would like."

Worcester had made Mattie the right offer, especially after his long paddle up the bay. Two of Mattie's favourite things were "live" tea, with lots of sugar, and fresh homemade bread.

Worcester had not come by this information by accident. He had shared a couple of evening meals with Frank and Millie while waiting for Mattie to show up. They had told him many things about their "favourite Injun." They could say nothing bad about him. Millie had given Mattie many loaves of her bread, she told Worcester.

"Mind you, I should not 'ave said give. 'Cause many's a time he has tossed a good meal of trout upon the wharf on his way back up the arm. And sometimes deer meat, too, though I never once asked fer anyt'ing fer me loaf of bread." The kind-hearted woman clearly like Mattie Mitchell. Worcester trusted her judgment of the Indian.

Worcester and Mattie talked about fishing and hunting over

two cups of hot tea in the warm forecastle. The American didn't mention his desire to find pearls. When Mattie had finished the last cup of tea, along with several well-buttered slices of Millie's bread, and mixed the tea dregs with sugar and had eaten that as well, he agreed to guide Worcester on a trip up the coast.

During his time with Frank over the next few days, Worcester became convinced the man had tuberculosis. Worcester was not a doctor, but he was a learned man and had seen many such cases. He carefully broached the subject to Frank privately one late, quiet evening while they sat on the bridge leading to his kitchen door. They were no less than 100 feet beyond the wharf where the schooner pulled gently at her moorings.

Frank looked around to see if Millie was near before he answered. They heard her inside the house busily cleaning up after their delicious evening meal. "You're probably right about dat, Reveran'," he said quietly. Both Frank and Millie refused to call him by any other name when they found out he was a man of the cloth.

Frank was smoking a short-stemmed pipe that he had filled with the rich-smelling American tobacco Worcester had brought. The good reverend liked a few draws from his own well-used briar after a good supper.

Frank had just finished his usual bout of coughing followed by a round of spitting. He always coughed more after a few lungfuls of pipe smoke. Worcester mentioned this to him. Frank coughed again and, when he was able to speak again, said in a low voice, "The TB is bad 'ere, Reveran', all 'long the coast and 'round the island too. Dere's hundreds of people dead from it, I 'ear."

Frank looked toward the kitchen window, fearing Millie would hear him. "She fears the same as I do, ya know. Not stupid, is my Millie. We don't talk about it much. We'll be leavin' fer Canada now in a few days. Goin' up where me son is. 'Twas why

I sold me scunner. Fer the passage money an' a few dollars to have in me pocket when I gets dere. 'Tis easy fer a man good wit' his 'ands to get good paying work up dere, me boy sez. 'Ouses gettin' built up ever'where. I can do dat. Built dis one, I did." He pointed to the neat home behind them.

"Dere's more dan dat, too. Good doctors up dere. Our boy told us dat in a letter we got from 'im. Dey'll fix me up fer sure. Dere's a big lake where Danny lives, jest as big as the gulf out dere, he says."

Here Frank pointed beyond the long, indented bay toward the hidden Gulf of St. Lawrence and continued. "'Twill break me 'eart to leave me cove, ya know. Millie's nephew is taking over me 'ouse. Dey jes' got married. Only to live in, ya know. An tek care of while we're gone. I'm not selling me 'ouse. After I'm feelin' better I'll be back again. Can't let me 'ouse an' lan' go. Wot's a man got to come back to wit' nar 'ouse and not even a piece of lan' lef' to call 'is own?"

As usual, Frank said what he had to say in his usual fast-talking manner without stopping. The hand that held his slow-burning pipe did all of his gesticulating this time. With every swing of his arm, toward the bay or his home or the white-curtained kitchen window, puffs of blue smoke trailed away from the bowl of the pipe.

He stopped to cough again. Worcester waited, expecting him to start talking again. But he didn't continue. He just stared at the schooner that was no longer his, which kept tugging at her lines with a soft rubbing sound. Once, Frank's hand brushed along both his eyes with his usual quick, animated movement.

Worcester knew that Frank and Millie's son, Danny, had left to find work in Toronto last fall. The boy wanted something different, a weeping Millie had told him.

"Broke his father's 'eart, Danny B'y did—an' me own, too,

watchin' me only chil' walk down 'longshore and 'eaded away from us. 'Twas some 'ard, b'y—excuse me, sir . . . Reveran', I mean to say."

Danny had left after the summer's fishing was done. His parents, who loved their only child too much to deny him a different and likely better future than the one that lay before them, "scrimped" together enough money for their boy's passage. Now, with a good paying job and a place of his own, he wanted his parents to join him. Worcester felt the pain this simple loving couple relayed to him over their son's leaving. Now, staring out the bay, Worcester avoided looking at his new friend sitting beside him and wisely said nothing.

CHAPTER 8

MATTIE MITCHELL AND ELWOOD WORCESTER left Humber Arm at daybreak two days later. Standing at the wharf and waving a tearful farewell—not to the two men, but to the boat that he would never see again and that he still considered his—stood Frank. Only when the *Danny Boy* cleared the wharf head and turned her stern to the land did Worcester see a parted upstairs curtain where a nightgown-clad Millie watched the leaving schooner without waving.

They sailed out the long bay under a grey dawning sky. There was barely enough wind to gather the mainsail, but the two men were in no hurry. The schooner came out from under the mountain shadows as she slipped toward the sea, and soon the flat mountains released the yellow sun until full daylight was upon the land and the sea.

For Mattie Mitchell it was an awesome first. He loved the experience of standing on the deck of a free-sailing schooner. His canoe was secured to the slightly tilted deck of the schooner with its river-scarred bottom facing up. Many times over the years he had used a small makeshift sail while canoeing this very bay or crossing large inland lakes. Usually his jacket or a blanket served such a purpose. But here on the deck of a huge vessel, he marvelled at the feeling of gliding effortlessly along. However, as was his way, he did not volunteer his thoughts to Worcester.

His keen eye and quick mind followed Worcester's every move as the man brought the vessel under full sail. The American patiently explained the workings as he did so. Long before they reached the open Gulf of St. Lawrence, Mattie understood enough to aid Worcester with the running of the boat.

It was when Worcester asked Mattie to try his hand at steering the boat that he learned more about the Indian and his people. This was how the American would find out much more about the man he would grow to love and respect for the rest of his life.

"How about taking the helm for a while, Mattie?" Worcester asked, indicating the wheel held firmly in his grip. Without the slightest hesitation, and not asking the American why he had called it a helm, Mattie Mitchell grasped the polished dowelled spokes and with a confident air stood before his first mast.

Standing away from the wheel and giving Mattie full control of the vessel, Worcester explained to him what Frank had warned him about. Long after Worcester had paid for the *Danny Boy*, an apologetic Frank had told Worcester his one complaint about the little schooner.

"She yaws a bit to port, she does. You must forever kep a strong 'an' on the starburd spokes, else she'll veer port, she will. I suspec' 'tis a bit of want in her keel is causin' it. I fergot to tell 'e about it before. Do ya want yer money back?"

Worcester smiled at the memory and told Mattie that Frank had told him the truth. The schooner did indeed "yaw a bit to port," especially if the wheel was left unattended for a moment. If Frank had not mentioned it, Worcester simply would have considered it as part of the schooner's handling. He found no other fault with his schooner.

Standing tall and proud at the wheel and with the open sea

coming into view, Mattie wondered if he would get the seasickness he had heard so much about. He never did.

Worcester was delighted with his new guide. He immediately saw the intelligence of the man. The way he grasped the workings of a sailing vessel with little tutoring impressed him greatly. It was something many men found difficult to understand, even after spending months at sea. Yet the Indian became a capable hand before the first day was done.

Worcester also noticed how Mattie looked him full in the eyes when he was talking to him. It was as if the man was seeing into his very thoughts, giving him his full attention. It was the reason Mattie learned so quickly. Worcester would also come to know that any time Mattie paid no attention to him, it meant he wasn't interested in the subject. At such times Mattie listened quietly but always looked away, his body language showing his lack of interest.

On this day, standing on the deck of the schooner that carried them out to the blue sea, a friendship began that would last the lifetimes of both men. It was the start of years of adventure that would take them along hundreds of shady woodland trails and through many secluded inland waterways. With a proud Mattie at the wheel, they scunned out the long bay, with the schooner's forefoot disturbing the water along the shadowed edge of the high, tabletop mountains as they went.

They came up under the lee of Woods Island at the mouth of the arm with a bright sun beaming on the neat, colourful houses of the fisher people living there. Small dories filled the water around the island, most of them a rich vermilion, the single oarsmen paddling along. With friendly waves to the industrious boats as they passed, the schooner sailed on across the open mouths of the middle and then north arms of the Bay of Islands.

Worcester frequently consulted the schooner compass as they

journeyed out the bay. Having no map of the area, he trusted to Mattie's directions. When Mattie pointed the way they should take to cross the bay, Worcester pointed the bow of the *Danny Boy* in that direction. Looking into the wooden binnacle, he told Mattie they were sailing due north and 290 degrees toward the west.

Mattie watched the compass spin slowly as the schooner veered. Showing his trademark disinterest, he turned away. "I don't know 'bout that stuff, Preacher. I know North Star. My people always follow drinking gourd. You find North Star, you find all stars. Din you find your way. It is nuff fer me."

Worcester nodded thoughtfully at the wisdom of this statement and grinned at the moniker the Indian had attached to him. On the very first day of their meeting, Worcester had mentioned that he was an ordained minister of the Episcopalian faith. Mattie hadn't heard that term before, and when Worcester tried to explain that he was like a priest, Mattie shook his head.

"You like no priest I see. No long dress like woman. You more like preacher man."

And so it was that Mattie called Worcester "Preacher." And after a few failed attempts at telling Mattie he could call him Elwood or Worcester, or even Reverend if he wanted to, he gave up and accepted his new name. For the rest of their time together Mattie would call him nothing else, and always the name was said with the respect the man had for the clergy. After a while he became known around the bay as Mattie's preacher, and Worcester came to like the title.

They had put Woods Island behind them and were well across the mouth of the bay, which Worcester figured might be ten or so miles wide, when he saw something that amazed him. They were passing by one of the small fishing boats. The lone fisherman standing in the stern of the dory had a long sculling oar in his left hand. It passed between two vertical thole-pins in the centre of the craft and entered the water at a jaunty angle.

The fisherman held the other end of the oar in the crook of his arm and regularly twisted it in a circular motion that appeared to keep the bow of the boat into the light wind. The man standing straight and tall with the long oar reminded Worcester of a Venetian gondolier.

But it was another, more unusual action that fascinated the American. The fisherman was constantly bending to and fro from the waist up. In the same determined motion, with his right hand he kept pulling and releasing nothing. It was only when they sailed closer that they could see a line running out over the gunnel of the boat.

The American had never seen such a method of fishing before. The fisherman's hand came to a sudden, jolting stop on its upward pull. In an instant the man drew the long oar across the thwarts of the boat, grasped the line with both hands, and began pulling in a fluid, vigorous hand-over-hand motion. In the space of just a couple of minutes he yanked a shiny white codfish over the side, flicked a large hook from its mouth, threw the hook over the side again, and, as the line ran back down into the sea, grabbed the sculling oar and spun the boat—which had turned broadside—into the gentle wind once more. It was all done with the speed and dexterity of a man who excelled at his trade. The fisherman looked toward the passing schooner, waved his friendly right hand on the upstroke, and quickly bent over again to pull another glistening fish out of the water.

Worcester asked Mattie if the fish were so plentiful that they could be caught just anywhere.

"No. Only on good grounds feesh caught. Dat man good fisherman. Always wave to me. He know *Danny B'y*. He know grounds ver' well, too."

Worcester asked if "grounds" were the same as banks, to which Mattie replied he was pretty sure that they were.

"But how does he know where these underwater grounds are?" asked Worcester. "Does he use a chart and compass?"

"No compass. 'E use landmarks for feesh grounds. I show you ver' soon," answered the ever-patient Mattie, who was carefully studying the distant land as he spoke.

Soon, at Mattie's request they dropped the sails. The schooner slowed and finally lost its headway. Mattie produced his own hook and line like the one they had seen the fisherman using. They found another one aboard the schooner. The big hooks were embedded into the heads of a grey moulded lead fish close to six inches in length. A heavy line was tied to its tail. Mattie scraped the sides of the fish with his knife until the lure shone like new.

Unwinding the line from its wooden reel, he threw the jigger over the side and watched it glint and finally disappear into the green depths. When the line went slack in his hands, indicating it had reached bottom, Mattie hurriedly pulled it back several feet. In less than a minute a large cod lay flopping for life on the deck of the drifting schooner. Mattie threw the jigger back over the side. As it sang over the broad bulwark, he grabbed the thrashing fish, cut its narrow, white throat, grasped the bottomed-out line, and reset it as before.

Worcester watched it all in stunned silence. Under Mattie's watchful eye he soon had his own line over the side. After a few jigs he pulled out of the water a struggling fish of his own.

"You cut feesh throat, maybe. Make better taste wit' blood gone," Mattie advised.

Worcester took the knife and, after finally getting a grip on the slippery, writhing fish, began to cut its throat.

"You don't cut to kill. You cut to bleed. Feesh 'eart keep

pumping till all blood leave. Ver' much better taste. You see soon," Mattie said in his usual advisory tone of voice. Worcester understood the reasoning and did as he was told.

While they fished, Worcester asked Mattie to explain to him how they had found the fishing shoals by using landmarks. Mattie illustrated a simple yet clever method of using points of land aligned with another point—or a mountain, or a sky-lining tree, or someone's white house—as marks to find good fishing spots below the sea.

They soon had several fish aboard and promptly cut the throat of each one. A pool of blood stained the schooner's otherwise clean deck by the time they had finished. Mattie looked toward the land at his two sets of landmarks.

"We drif' off mark. Dis boat drif' ver' fas'. Mus' come 'round to mark again. We 'ave nuff feesh. Maybe we go now."

Worcester agreed with Mattie, as he always would to his subtle suggestions. They hauled the sails aloft again, and the schooner gained way with her bows pointing a little east of north, tacking its way toward the north arm of Bay of Islands. Behind them the land closed so that there appeared to be no way into the deep fjord from which they had just sailed. And high above it all spread the snow-capped escarpments of the Long Range Mountains.

They cooked the codfish in the small galley as they sailed, and ate their fill of the sweet flesh on the open, sun-drenched deck of the bustling little schooner after they had tied her helm. And while the two men supped, the fragrant summer wind came and gently luffed the sails, providing music for the passengers of the *Danny Boy*.

Ever curious, Worcester asked the names of the islands and headlands they passed. Mattie gladly replied, calling out the name of each place of interest. The bay itself seemed to be shielded from the gulf by a string of islands that ran parallel to the inner coastline.

When Mattie told Worcester the names of two of the islands were Guernsey and Tweed, the American pointed out that they were also island names from the English Channel. They were the names of sheep's wool found on these far-off islands. In fact, he had a fine guernsey sweater below in his duffle bag.

But it was the name of another island that really got the American's full attention: Big Pearl Island. Here was the perfect opportunity to tell Mattie Mitchell the real reason for his visit to the west coast of Newfoundland.

Worcester told Mattie the story about the Cabots who had discovered Newfoundland. Mattie's eyes narrowed and he turned away from him.

"Who discover? My people 'ere long before dat time. White man come without ask. Take many hunting lands. Net rivers and ponds, too. Salmon ver' plenty before. White man put dem in barrels. Make dem stink wit' salt. Not many salmon like before dis time." Mattie spoke without looking at his companion.

Worcester saw the sudden change in the man and felt his quiet anger. He would never again underestimate his intelligence or his sensitivity. He apologized for his remark. The Indian was fiercely proud of his ancestry. Mattie was back to his amiable self again, and when Worcester told him about John Cabot giving the pearls to the king of England, Mattie posed one of his rare questions.

"How come, English man, no one ever see king of dis lan'?"

Worcester stared into the curious face of a man who really expected him to give a suitable answer and realized he had no answer that Mattie would understand. For the first time in his life, Worcester realized who really owned the lands they had fought over. He had no explanation to give.

Mattie threw a picked-clean sound from one of the cod over

the side and watched a lone gull circle for the white bone. The Indian was still thinking about kings. He spoke again in his usual direct manner.

"We have ver' many kings. We call dem chiefs. No Europe mans ever respec' our chiefs. Ver' first Mi'kmaq dey meet in Acadie is king. 'Is woman wit' 'im, too. She be queen if she white. Still no respec'." Mattie looked directly into Worcester's eyes as he made his thoughtful statements.

Worcester had no way of knowing it, but Mattie Mitchell was right. In 1597, on Cape Breton Island, Itary was the first recorded Mi'kmaq to meet with the Europeans. They recorded him as "king" and his woman—whom they did not name—as queen. But above and below the historical entry, they were both referred to as "mere savages."

They talked more then, as men will. And for both men it was a time of learning. Mattie told Worcester stories handed down for generations by the Saywedikiks—the ancients—of the Mi'kmaq people: of restless young Mi'kmaq men who had made their way across Acadie to the big western bay of great tides that the white men call Fundy; of how they had crossed this bay and followed the coastline south and entered the mouths of many mighty rivers; of one river called Missacipee far to the southwest that flowed out of an endless land, a river that was so long they found no end to it, even after two moons of searching. While the men talked, the soft summer wind came up out of the gulf and bore them gently to the north side of Bay of Islands.

There came a lull in their talk, and when Worcester figured Mattie's mind was again in the present, he changed the subject completely and asked, "Is it possible to find blue mussels and/ or lobster around these shores, Mattie? It is a delicacy I dearly love."

"Ver' many mussels ever'where. We get pot full easy at low

tide. Best time full moon. Full moon, full mussel shell. We use cod guts fer lobster bait. We hook dem ver' easy."

Although Worcester relished the idea of a pot filled with the tasty delicacies, his mind was on another type of shellfish. He decided to be as direct as his guide and speak his mind. "What about freshwater mussels or clams, Mattie? Have you seen any of them in the rivers hereabouts?"

Mattie replied without hesitation "Ver' many black mussels in many rivers. Brooks, too. Dey no good fer grub. Dey stink ver' bad when cookin'. Why you eat dem ones? Only muskrat eat dem ones."

Worcester chuckled at the face Mattie made when talking about the mussels but quickly reassured him that he didn't want them for food. He wanted them for the pearls that they may contain. Again Mattie answered right away.

"Ver' many small pearls. Some big ones. Most grey ones. Some white ones."

The wind faded away as early summer breezes sometimes do and the sails slacked and slumped a bit when the strength went out of them. Worcester walked aft over the spotless deck and started to tighten the sheets in an effort to take up the slack. Mattie joined him and released the big wheel from its fetters to steer the *Danny Boy* toward the closing land.

For two more days the American and what he now considered his Indian friend sailed and explored part of the western coast of Newfoundland in the trim little schooner. And in all of that time Worcester pumped the bilge only once. Frank had said it right. The salt sea waters had plimmed the schooner and she didn't leak.

They ate their fill of cod and mussels and lobster pulled from the blue gulf waters by day, and slept like babes in the cradle of bunks in the *Danny Boy* by night. The wind from the Gulf of St. Lawrence stayed in their favour until late one evening, when

Mattie steered the schooner into the black shadows of a high, sheltered cove.

"We leave scunner dis place, maybe. We use canoe after. Find ver' many black mussels. Big pearls, too, maybe."

They paddled ashore in Mattie's canoe as they had been doing for the past several nights, but for Worcester this night was different. Mattie's idea to leave the schooner unattended for several days was obviously the right one, but Worcester was reluctant to leave his boat. The tiny cove Mattie had chosen would keep the schooner safe from any wind, but it wasn't that. Worcester feared having his schooner, or at least the property he would have to leave aboard, stolen. He voiced his concern to Mattie.

"Ever'one know you wit' me. Ever'one know Frank's *Danny B'y*. No man steal from me." Mattie seemed unconcerned and went about starting their evening campfire.

Worcester was secretly unconvinced about a wandering stranger's honesty. He had a good sum of American money in his duffle bag, all of the money in small bills. For some reason that he couldn't explain, he didn't tell Mattie about the money. He decided he wouldn't leave the money behind but would take it with him.

Their evening meal consisted of freshly caught cod, which they cooked in a pot with less than an inch of salt water. In less than twenty minutes, Mattie dumped the boiled contents onto a flat rock. Along with the last of Millie's bread, both men ate until they were full.

Mattie added small pieces of grey-white driftwood to the dying fire. The shadowed schooner swung and creaked on her hook. The campfire brightened the cove, and for a brief time its yellow light shone across the night water and reached partway up the port side of the moored vessel.

Worcester poked tobacco into the bowl of his briar, tamped it tight with a broad thumb, pulled a thin, hot brand from the fire, and lit his pipe. When the tobacco started to glow, he settled back. A blue stream of smoke issued from his unshaven jaws and escaped out of his long nose. He spoke with the pipe clenched between his strong white teeth.

"She surely is a fine vessel, you know. Frank did not 'gyp' me, that's for sure. I know Frank's attachment to the boat was quite different from my own, but I have already come to love the *Danny Boy*. And I believe you have enjoyed our little sailing excursion as well, Mattie."

Mattie was looking at the schooner, too. He seemed to be considering something. Worcester waited. When Mattie spoke, his voice was soft and blended with the night sounds.

"My grandfather 'ave boat like *Danny B'y*, too. King of France give him scunner. King give king gif'."

Worcester was astonished at this revelation and prompted Mattie to tell him more of his history. After his usual careful thinking, Mattie continued.

His people had always lived here, he said. They were hunter-gatherers. The ancients called this island Taqamkuk and came across the "south water" from Acadie. The white man came across the great ocean to the east and, because they had not seen this land before, called it a "new" land. The Mi'kmaq passed their history down through the ages orally, but because their words were not on paper, the white man called them liars. Here Mattie was quick to point out the many treaties the Europeans had signed on their yellow papers.

They had taken great nations of land that wasn't theirs to take, in some cases doing so without consulting the native people, whom they considered had given them the land.

"White man lie wit' tongue. Lie wit' quill," said Mattie.

The very first chief of Taqamkuk was Mattie's great-grandfather, Michel Agathe. He was a Saqamaw, a very great and important chief who came from a long line of chieftains. He was respected by his people all along the south and west coasts of the island. His name was spoken the French way, Michel. The English, who hated everything French, and who couldn't pronounce it right anyway, changed Mattie's surname from Michel to Mitchell.

"French king give my grandfadder sloop as gif'. Just like *Danny B'y*, maybe?" Mattie continued.

Mattie's grandfather was called Captain Jock and also King Mitchell, depending on who you talked to at the time. Worcester answered Mattie's question quickly, wanting to hear more about the man's fascinating past.

"A sloop is a boat with one mast instead of two, Mattie."

Mattie acknowledged the answer with a look at the *Danny Boy*. The schooner had just turned broadside with the leaving tide. The tips of her two masts scratched the sky.

The king from faraway France had bestowed upon Mattie's ancestor a great gift. It was a rare thing for anyone to give an Indian anything, though Mattie figured the French ruler wanted to trade it for the locations of the best coastal fishing grounds and all the hidden reefs. In his new boat, King Jock was now called Captain Jock, a title more prestigious around the coast of nineteenth-century Newfoundland.

The French learned from Captain Jock not only where to find cod, their best market product, but many other new world commodities. The Mi'kmaq captain showed them white beaches in secluded coves where capelin came in late spring. He knew the rivers with the biggest runs of salmon in summer. He knew every brook where shiny smelt could be caught in the spring and the autumn.

The clever Frenchmen gained much more than that from the proud captain. At their "king's" command, native trappers passed the best of furs into French hands at the end of every winter season. The French learned the secrets of the countless forbidding bays and coves that defined this part of the coast. They gained infinite knowledge of the mysterious forested land, all in exchange for one wooden sloop.

His father, Mattie said, was a blooded Mi'kmaq named Jean Michael, whom the English called Jack or John Mitchell. At one time he lived in Conne River, a place were Mi'kmaq people found sanctuary from both French and English conquerors. It was situated at the end of a long bay that reached far inland. From Conne River, those who knew the way could follow meandering waterways into the vast interior of Newfoundland. Its entrance from the open sea was a puzzle of islands and deep canyons and dead-end arms that served as a deterrent to any would-be invaders.

Among the Mi'kmaq people John Mitchell was also known as King Mitchell. Like his father, he was a well-respected chieftain. His mother was the daughter of an Abenaki Indian who called the Abenaki "The Dawn People." Her father was John Stevens, who led the first of the Mi'kmaq to Halls Bay, where Mattie had been born.

Mattie's voice took on a measure of pride as he spoke of his ancestry. Worcester felt as though Mattie was pleased to talk to a white man who was listening. Mattie brought up his language again, as if he were sorry he couldn't speak English very well and that maybe Worcester wasn't understanding all that he was saying.

"When I speak only some of deir English words dey call me stupid man. When I speak my own words dey call me stupid man."

Worcester sensed he would hear no more about Mattie Mitchell's history on this night. "Mattie, I have studied in many places. I am considered to be a very educated man. I can speak no other language but my own. Yet you, who have had no schooling, and without being taught, can speak fluently not only your own wonderful language, but also English, which is considered to be the most difficult of all languages to learn. I can understand you very well. You have nothing to be ashamed of and a great deal to be proud of."

Worcester stood to stretch his cramped legs. He suddenly thought of one of the long-winded professors who had taught him. The man could have used some of Mattie Mitchell's direct way of speaking. If he had, Worcester thought, he could have stayed awake during his boring lectures. The American smiled at the thought and looked around the still cove. His gaze took in the firelight reflected across the black water.

"You know, Mattie," he said sincerely, "if your skin were white, you would be considered as royalty."

And Mattie Mitchell, who was the direct descendant of a legendary line of kings, walked away from the firelight to gather more driftwood. When he entered the shadows, he smiled at the thought.

CHAPTER 9

THE WIND DIED AND THE COVE blackened in deep shadow. The gentle motion from the tide lapped against the sloping shingle. From where the two men lay sprawled on the beach, only the tips of the schooner's masts were visible against the night sky. Worcester pulled on his pipe and found only the foul, burnt taste of ash remaining. He tapped the bowl of the briar against one of the rocks that lined their fireplace and watched the dottle fall among the glowing driftwood's ashes.

Mattie watched the preacher man pull a small, round, brass land compass out of his pocket and look into the north sky.

"You told me your people always use the North Star for guidance, Mattie. I know where north is, but I always have trouble finding the North Star itself. It isn't very bright, is it?"

"No, Nort' Star ver' faint. You know where Big Dipper is?" asked Mattie, and when Worcester assured him that he did indeed, Mattie, looking up into the firmament, spoke again. "Find Nort' Star easy with two fingers dis way."

There are seven stars in the Big Dipper and also seven stars in the little one, Mattie told him. Worcester had to admit he had never counted them before. The fire crackled and the small waves brushed against the beach. A snipe hunted somewhere high above them. The warbling sound escaped from its folded wings and echoed around the cove as it dived for moths. Pointing skyward, the easy-talking woodsman explained to the educated American how simple it was to get direction from the night heavens. Fascinated, Worcester watched and listened and saw right away what all of his book knowledge had never taught him.

With his long, brown fingers Mattie demonstrated to Worcester the age-old method of finding the Dog Star. Like an eager student, Worcester followed his every move. With the thumb of his right hand on the lower star and with his forefinger extended to reach the star above—Mattie called it the pointing star—which formed the outer edge of the Big Dipper opposite its handle, Mattie moved both fingers straight up five times, always keeping the fingers the same distance apart.

"Now pointing finger on firs' star in Little Dipper 'andle. Dis is Nort' Star. Never fail. My people use on land an' water. When one dipper empty, udder one always full." Mattie dropped his hand and watched as Worcester raised his own hand above his head to study this method of navigation. When he thanked Mattie for showing him the stars, adding that many of the old ways were still good ones, the Indian simply replied in his matter-of-fact way.

"If old way not good way, 'ow dey get old?" Worcester, who had no answer for such wisdom, said nothing.

They left the *Danny Boy* in the grey dawn of the following day. The schooner swung on her hook, with lots of scoop given. With two heavy lines running from the shore to each of her two sides, she looked secure in the narrow cove. Seated in Mattie's canoe, they made their way along the coast. In the stern of the craft and paddling on the left side sat the lean Indian. Seated in the bow and paddling on the right was the broad American preacher.

Between the two men sat their stored accoutrements and enough basic provisions to provide for days. A tan-coloured tent sat atop the pile, and two fly fishing rods stretched across the tent. Among their supplies were a double-barrelled shotgun in a waterproof case and Mattie's long bow. Next to the latter was a leather quiver filled with long arrows. Worcester had seen him put the weapon aboard but had not said anything about it. He was excited about seeing it put to use.

With each stroke and dip of the paddles, the canoe slid quickly along the coast. They rounded a point and left the *Danny Boy* in its sheltered cove behind. When the sun finally broached the mountains, grey clouds moved in to cover it.

"Clouds low. Rain dis day, maybe," Mattie said softly from the stern of the canoe.

Worcester agreed with his guide and shifted his paddle to the left side of the canoe. Behind him, Mattie changed to the right side. It is the way of paddlers, who know that a change is as good as a rest. Even without the sun the day was warm. The wind here was light, but a brisk wind threatened from the gulf. Before they had gone far, the wind had reached them, and waves came as if from nowhere and slapped against the side of the little craft, causing it to roll dangerously.

They were no more than a few feet from the formidable limestone coastline. Worcester was worried. He could see nowhere to go for shelter. He was about to voice his concern when the bow of the canoe suddenly turned in to the face of the cliffs. For a moment he thought they would capsize and grabbed both gunnels of the canoe.

"Keep paddlin'," came a low growl from the stern.

Worcester dipped his paddle into a surge of water that was rolling level with the gunnels. He held his breath in fear but kept paddling as instructed. Just when he was sure they would be thrown against the looming cliff face, the canoe gently lifted from behind and shot through a narrow passage with amazing speed.

And then they sped away from the scud of wind as they entered a long, pleasant arm where the big waves of the gulf could not reach. Worcester felt ashamed of himself for letting go of the paddle. It was a very dangerous thing to do. He said so to Mattie, who replied simply, "You do better nex' time." Worcester, hoping there would never be a next time, dug his paddle in deep as the canoe glided down a calm, pristine water valley. There would be many more narrow escapes for Worcester and his fearless guide, but the American would never again let go of his paddle.

They heard the brook running into the sea long before they saw it. It made its way into the sea through a flat, rocky, and very shallow delta. They hauled the canoe along the foundered banks, and at the first turn in the river the sea was gone from their view. They paddled across deep steadies, and up rattles they pulled their craft.

They fished and caught high-jumping Atlantic salmon in the intertidal pools. They caught flashing steelheads, which were in the same river and which Worcester had not fished before. As the two men had enjoyed the bounties of the rolling ocean before, now they relished the days and the taste of the wilderness.

Worcester had always figured himself to be a good fly fisherman. He was good at catching trout, but he was embarrassed with the pitiful results of his salmon catch in comparison to Mattie's. The man not only knew where the salmon were lying, he was always able not only to "rise" one of the fish, but promptly hook one. He pointed out to Worcester where to find the fish, but try as he might, the American could not get the hang of Atlantic salmon fly fishing.

They were at the end of a long, deep pool one late evening

casting for salmon. A salmon would jump out of the water at regular intervals and glisten as it turned to re-enter the water with a noisy splash.

Worcester tried his best to ward off the hordes of blackflies. They always seemed to hunt him more than they did his companion. He was having no success with his fishing and it put him in a foul mood. He called out to Mattie, who was just now removing the hook from his second salmon.

"Mattie, are you sure there are salmon behind these rocks? I have seen no sign of them there and I have changed flies several times without any luck whatsoever."

Mattie laid his own rod down, walked over to Worcester, and asked him for his rod. After studying the water for a minute or so, he made a long, slow cast. The line swung high and curved in a graceful arc that seemed to defy the wind, then gently landed the hook behind the same rock with which the American was trying his luck. A dark swirl of water appeared behind the hook. Mattie pulled quickly, but it came back empty.

"Dat one smart salmon," he said. "I try nex' one, maybe."

He cast his line toward another rock behind which he had told Worcester several salmon were waiting. The line presented the hook as before, and on the very next cast the same dark swirl of water appeared behind the moving fly. This time Mattie's pole snapped back with a rapid motion of his wrist, there was a sudden buzzing sound from the reel, a salmon jumped for freedom, the tiny reel gears clicked, the rod bent from tip to middle, and the play began. Mattie landed his fish, cast a few more times behind each of the two rocks, and raised two more salmon. He handed the rod back to Worcester.

"I catch one salmon fer you, show you t'ree more. Now your turn again."

With that he started to walk back to his own fishing spot.

Worcester couldn't understand what he was doing wrong. He pleaded with Mattie.

Mattie turned and said, "You cast ver' good line. You don't watch hook. Your eye mus' never leave hook. Watch fer willum. Den pull quick."

Worcester didn't have any idea what a "willum" was and didn't know why he had to keep his eye on the hook. In his usual patient way, Mattie Mitchell explained to the preacher the secret of fly fishing for the wily Atlantic salmon. The salmon came in out of the ocean to these swift rivers to spawn, he said, not to feed. He had gutted many of them late in the season. Their bellies were always empty, even though the water surface was alive with many kinds of insects. Why they didn't feed, he wasn't sure, nor did he care. He just knew what he saw.

When the fish rose for the hook, it wasn't for food. He told Worcester that when he saw the "willum," or swirl, directly behind his trailing hook, the salmon already had the hook in its mouth. That was the instant to set the hook. The fish would spit the metal out of its mouth quicker than it had taken it. Worcester admitted to Mattie that he had always waited for a bite as if he were fishing for trout. Mattie told him again, "No willum, no salmon. Feel him take, too late."

Worcester never took his eye from the hook again. His salmon fishing improved, but he could never match the skill of Mattie Mitchell. Worcester always believed that Mattie had another secret to fishing, and, like all fishermen, kept it to himself.

* * * * *

FOR THIS EXPEDITION THEY HAD TAKEN one black cooking pot, a much smaller pot for tea, and an iron frying pan. Worcester cooked the red salmon over an open fire near the water where it had been caught. Mattie cut the steelhead down the back, opened up its thick sides with several lateral cuts, and placed the fillets flesh down on flat rocks close to the fire. When the salmon had sizzled to a golden brown and the trout started to emit sweet-smelling steam out of every cut, both men began eating. They exchanged pieces of fish. Worcester loved the naturally cooked trout best. But Mattie Mitchell wanted something more. He wanted meat.

On they moved up the river, which narrowed, widened, and ran deep and shallow, until they came to a place where the river was almost lost in low boglands. They quietly paddled through a place with tall green grasses. Two or more small streams meandered out of the grasses and joined the bigger river. Mattie guided the canoe into one of the narrowest of these leads. A bend appeared, and beyond it the tributary seemed to widen into a circular pond. The long-stemmed grasses grew everywhere here.

Worcester felt Mattie shift his paddle, and in the next instant the boat turned and slid in among the tall goose grass. They were now parallel to the slow stream. Worcester was surprised to feel a firm, gravelly bottom at the end of his paddle. He turned to ask a question but heard "No turn, no talk."

For a long time they waited, for what Worcester had no idea. Once, he felt a slight movement and heard a faint rustle from the back of the canoe. He did not turn around. Their heads barely topped the grass. Worcester thought the blossoming grass ends would grow into wild rice, but he wasn't sure and dared not ask.

The stream beside them appeared still and black like a mirror. There was nothing to see of the water save for the slight bend just ahead of them. Presently, two small objects at the bend in the water came into the American's view. At first he thought it was something that had been floating there before and he hadn't noticed. But then another object appeared from below the water.

As he watched, three more heads broke the surface, and then all five muskrat swam toward them, with a tiny, V-shaped wake following them.

All five of the rodents stopped less than fifteen yards from the hidden canoe, and two of them started swimming in wide, slow circles. The wobbling sound of air escaping the wings of an airborne snipe hunting for summer moths came to them from high above. Worcester looked skyward, hoping to see it. He had always loved the sound. He spotted the snipe hundreds of feet in the air. Suddenly it dived earthward for something Worcester couldn't see, and the same high-pitched wilderness sound burst forth.

Worcester turned back to the muskrats. There were only two to be seen. He looked all around but could not see the others. A few minutes passed and they appeared again, bobbing up from the water like black corks. They swam toward the opposite shore, hauled themselves onto a low, sloped rock, and began eating. They were eating clams.

Still no sound or movement came from Mattie. The muskrats on the rock finished the clams and, slid into the water one by one. They swam out into the stream and dived below the surface again. The two larger muskrats, which had kept swimming around during this activity, suddenly dived in unison. One of the other heads appeared. There came at the same instant a sound like a suddenly released branch on a quiet trail. Worcester saw a long, slim arrow pass through the muskrat's throat where its soaked fur met the waterline.

The startled animal tried to dive, but it only managed to get half of its body below the water. Then, with the arrow sticking straight up out of its neck, it swam in slow circles until it slowed and finally stopped. Another head appeared and for a moment faced the canoe. Worcester heard the same gentle rush of air behind him, this time accompanied by the twang of Mattie's bow. Fascinated, he saw the arrow enter the muskrat's throat, heard a sudden squeal of pain from the creature's open mouth, then watched as its head fell forward in a frothy bubble of blood and water.

The other rodents surfaced and appeared to be alarmed. Worcester was waiting for at least the closest one to receive the same fate as the other two, when the Indian spoke loud and clear.

"We 'ave plen'y. We eat good dis night. Young muskrat taste ver' good. Tomorrow we find much clams. Maybe much pearls, too."

And then, just as Mattie had predicted, the rain began.

* * * * *

FOR AS LONG AS HE LIVED, ELWOOD WORCESTER would never forget that first night he spent with Mattie Mitchell in the true wilderness. Both of them were soaked by the time they had set up the tent and stowed their gear inside. Just around the bend from where Mattie had killed the two muskrats, a droke of fir, some spruce, and white birch jutting out from the wetlands provided a suitable campsite. Around the trees the ground was firm and level. The falling rain made the fir trees come alive with a sweet scent that hung in the air. Their fire, once Mattie got it really going just outside the tent's triangular door, gave off wisps of grey smoke that rose with the sparkling yellow flankers.

Worcester was no stranger to the ways of the wild, but this day and night would forever stand out as the time when he had really lived with nature. He had fished the salt sea and jigged codfish. He had taken salmon from the clear river waters. He had seen a man kill for food in the most primitive of ways. He was also pretty sure he was about to eat the flesh of muskrat. Above them, the ageless, dark mountains with all of their splendours kept a silent watch.

The rain stopped as suddenly as it had started. The air warmed in the windless night. The trees all around them divested themselves of the fallen water, dripping and plunking and plinking into the stream from overhanging branches, tapping on leaves and drumming on the ground. Away from the rim of firelight, the night was as black as pitch. Snipes hunted and cried above the two men. Somewhere a loon voiced its need, and from farther away its haunting cry was answered.

Mattie carefully skinned the two muskrats by the fire. He saved both of the dark brown pelts, though he told Worcester the hides were not at their best this time of year.

"Dis one yours," he told Worcester, indicating one of the naked pink carcasses. "You cook on stick or in iron pan?"

Worcester had some qualms about eating the scrawny meat cooked in any fashion and told Mattie so.

"Caribou meat. Bear meat. Water rat meat. All meat. Only taste is differen'," Mattie said quietly.

Worcester couldn't argue with that logic. Given the choice of frying his "rat" or roasting it over the campfire, and seeing Mattie's supper skewered and dangling over the fire, he suddenly realized he was famished. He picked up the meat and, as if having read his mind, Mattie handed him a stick for roasting.

"Good. We use fry pan fer bannock," Mattie said.

From his pack, which mysteriously seemed to contain many small and useful items, Mattie pulled a tin of bear fat. Worcester handed him the flour bag and Mattie stirred a measure of flour and brook water together. Greasing the pan with the heavy bear fat, he poured the pan more than half full with the moist dough.

While their evening meal cooked, both men prepared a drying rack near the fire. Worcester helped cut young saplings for their purpose. Mattie was impressed with the American, who always helped with every chore—except with the skinning.

Over the years he had taken many sportsmen into the wilds of Newfoundland. Many of them would not carry their own guns or their fancy fishing rods, but expected their guide to "do what he was paid to do."

One of them had taken Mattie's uncomplaining manner too far. The short, skinny man, who was always out of breath and who complained and whined at just about everything, had demanded Mattie carry him on his back across a knee-high brook. Without hesitating, Mattie sat on a low rock near the swift brook, the grumpy man climbed on his bent back, and off they went. Approaching midstream, where the brook was deepest, and without uttering a sound of warning, Mattie tripped and fell into the cold water, unceremoniously depositing his screaming passenger as he did so. The cries and terrible curse words from the sputtering man only increased as he waded and stumbled ashore—on the wrong side—and did not see the grin on the face of his proud guide.

The blue smoke rose from the campfire. Steam drifted upward from the drying clothing. The fat from the roasting meat dripped and sputtered down upon the glowing coals. The browning bannock bread smelled almost as good as Millie's loaves. The two loons called again to announce they had found each other. The high, rolling laughter of the triumphant male resounded through the hills. And then, as if on cue, a new sickle moon appeared above the southern hills. On its silvery back it carried the faint outline of the old one.

When the muskrats were cooked and just before the bannock started to burn, both men sat back and ate. When Worcester finished the last bite of his meat, he wiped the last of the bear fat drippings from the pan with a piece of bread. He sighed with pleasure and told Mattie the meat had a taste similar to chicken—only better. He even copied Mattie, who, after roasting the small leg bones on the hot coals, had cracked them open and ate the thin, yellow marrow inside. Walking to the brook, Worcester washed his hands and face, looked thoughtfully at the opening skies for a while, and stepped inside the tent to join his guide for a well-deserved rest.

* * * * *

"DIS DAY UQANTIE'UMG — SUNDAY, PREACHER," Mattie said after they had breakfasted the next morning. He looked at Worcester expectantly. Worcester saw in Mattie's hand a well-used prayer book that he had removed from a tooled leather bag. Mattie made the sign of the Cross over the book.

"And so it is, Mattie. I must apologize, for I had completely forgotten the day."

Seeing in Mattie's small, dark eyes the need for something more from him on this day, Worcester stood, bowed his head, and voiced aloud a prayer. He suddenly felt as though he were standing in the grandest of churches, with an audience of one giving him his rapt attention. When Worcester asked to see the Catholic prayer book, Mattie passed it to him. He admired the leather bag made to fit over it. Mattie explained to him the case was made from *babiche*, rawhide made from the well-tanned hide of a caribou.

The book had a red ochre colour and fit easily into the palm of Worcester's hand. He opened the book and was astonished to learn he could not read one word inside. The book was written in Mattie's own Mi'kmaq language! He asked Mattie if he could read and was totally surprised at the answer.

"Some. Not much. Ver' few words. No one show me my own tongue. No paper. Not even 'lowed to speak my own tongue. Dey call it savage talk. Dey laugh when I speak my talk. Dey laugh when I speak English talk."

Mattie told Worcester one white man had showed an interest in his language one time, but he only wanted him to say a few Mi'kmaq swear words. The man had waited with great expectation, a smirk on his bearded face. He couldn't wait to hear Mattie reveal the curse words so he could share them with his friends. But Mattie said, "My language 'ave no swear words. Only white man curse great spirit wit' swear words." The man had walked away, cursing angrily.

With his usual matter-of-fact attitude, Mattie explained to Worcester that he had attended school only briefly, where he was forbidden to speak the language of his people, where he was looked down upon and treated little better than a dog, and from which he left at a very early age and never returned. Worcester, ever the humanitarian, secretly equated Mattie's plight to that of the black people of his own country and felt ashamed.

Mattie shrugged off the things that had been, as was his way, and told Worcester how he came to read. He had guided two geologists, Alexander Murray and James Howley, for years. They were good men. Around dozens of campfires, especially in autumn when the nights were long, they had shown Mattie the basics of reading. Howley, especially, showed an interest in this endeavour and was very pleased to see Mattie read a few words. They had been friends for years. Mattie told Worcester that he had called Howley "Sage," his Mi'kmaq word for James, and Howley would call Mattie nothing else but Matthieu.

Still handling the well-worn prayer book, Worcester asked Mattie if he was a churchgoer and if he had ever been baptized. Mattie replied that he went to Mass sometimes, where he always sat in the back of the church. He only went when he felt like it, understood some of it, loved the mystery of it, and that he knew nothing about baptism. However, like all of his people, he had always been spiritual.

"My people have big M'n't'u spirit all 'round." Here Mattie spread his arms to indicate his surroundings. "Ver' many people not find M'n't'u outside church."

Worcester, who had been trained in a sectarian world and knew that Manitou was considered a Supreme Being with all of the native peoples, said nothing. Mattie put the book—which he would open every Sunday morning for as long as Worcester knew him—back inside its rawhide covering and got to his feet.

"Mass time over. We fin' pearls now, maybe."

Worcester, rising to his feet, said, "Amen."

* * * * *

HE ENTERED THE COLD WATER OF THE slow-moving stream to his knees. When Worcester offered to help, Mattie told him, "I fin' clams. You shuck 'em." Worcester agreed. He did not relish wading in cold water.

Twice Mattie brought his big hands above the water, filled with what he called freshwater mussels. He inspected them carefully and threw them back. The next time he brought only two, which were bigger than the others, their shells stained brown. They looked very old. These he tossed ashore to an excited Worcester, who broke them open. Inside one he found nothing, but deep inside the mucous body of the second one he found a white pearl as big around as the top of his finger. Mattie had found the clam bed and the pearls, as promised.

They stayed on that river for more than a week. Mattie retrieved clams from the cold water and never once complained. Nor did he appear to suffer from the frigid task. Every day, they spotted muskrat swimming toward them. Upon seeing the tall man throwing handfuls of clams upon the grassy bank, the animals turned back, disappointed, and quickly dived again, not breaking the surface again until they were much farther away.

They collected no less than 490 pearls of varying sizes and colours, only a few of which could compare with the first one they had found. Worcester deemed all of the dull-coloured, non-circular ones useless and threw them away. It was a big mistake. Months later, while meeting with a pearl merchant in New York City, Worcester learned much more about pearls.

The jeweller told him that the pearls sometimes kept growing in the clam long after it had become a threat to its body. The mollusk kept layering the pearl like an onion. Often inside the seemingly useless covering is the finest pearl of all. Further to this, during a trip to the Smithsonian Institute in Washington D.C., he learned that Mattie Mitchell had indeed been right about the relationship between muskrat and pearls. The muskrat, he was told by a knowledgeable curator, considers the clam a delicacy.

The muskrat is also the carrier of a water-borne parasite that is deadly to the freshwater mollusk. Diving among the sharp-edged open clams, there are times when the parasite is torn from the muskrat's sodden fur as it rips and tears the clams from their riverbeds. The rodent's parasite then sometimes becomes embedded inside the body of the clam. Unable to dislodge the invasion, the animal entombs and isolates the virus with its natural secretions, thus suffocating it. The resulting build-up of nacreous fluids hardens and holds the louse a prisoner forever. Without ever knowing the scientific reason why, Mattie Mitchell was intelligent enough to make the correlation.

The two men made their way down the river and out of the wilderness on a warm summer evening. They paddled in the gloaming to where the *Danny Boy* still waited. No one had been aboard during their absence. The day was just about spent, so, rather than sail out the bay in the dark, they spent the night aboard the schooner.

After sailing back to Bay of Islands and paying Mattie for his admirable services, Worcester set a date for an extended caribou hunt early in the autumn, hired two crewmen, and set sail for Labrador.

CHAPTER 10

AS PROMISED, ONE DAY IN THE LATTER PART of summer, the little *Danny Boy* came reaching up the bay and tied up at Frank's wharf. And Mattie Mitchell was waiting. They made arrangements for an extended stay, which would be spent on Mattie's favourite hunting grounds far inland. This time they would leave the schooner at Frank's wharf and paddle away from the community in the canoe.

On the last evening before their departure, Worcester was having his evening draw and was quietly walking the deck of his schooner, studying the heavens and remembering the lesson Mattie had taught him about the North Star. He was bending down to knock the dottle out of his pipe when he thought he saw a movement on the inside of the wharf. He waited for his night visitor to walk out over the wharf. But after several minutes, no one came.

Then he heard the sound of someone running along the narrow lane that paralleled the quiet cove. Glancing toward the sound, he caught only a glimpse of a fleeting shadow. The man's feet sounded hard on the gravel path as he ran. For some reason Worcester thought the runner had big feet. The shadow he saw was a tall one. Going below, he opened his portmanteau and counted out all of his remaining cash. Along with the money in his purse, he still had more than $500 in American bills. He put all of the money in his purse, stuffed it deep inside his duffle bag, and tied the mouth tight. The following morning he and Mattie paddled across the calm bay. Worcester said nothing about the money he carried and remained quiet about his unknown night visitor.

For three days they paddled up river and lake and finally reached the place where Mattie hunted. Mattie and Worcester successfully hunted and lived off the bountiful land for several days. Worcester had never seen a place like it. He would never have believed such a paradise existed if not for the fact that he had seen it with his own eyes.

Day after day they hunted and fished. Worcester killed several caribou, one of them a magnificent stag with more than forty points. Mattie made use of all of every carcass. He cooked the cleaned intestines, stuffed with meat, and roasted the stomach linings. He relished the entire viscera of each animal and took a particular liking to the kidneys. The Indian skinned the tongues and fried them in an iron pan. He heated the bones and ate the nourishing marrow inside.

Mattie dried and smoked the tender flesh of every doe and informed Worcester—after he had taken his trophy bull—that the stag meat "tasted ronky when 'orny." He cleaned and dried the caribou's bladders and used them as leak-proof containers. He scraped and flensed the best of the hides and then dried them in the cool autumn wind with their long hairs intact. Others he soaked in a mixture of ashes and water and then hung them to dry before working them into rawhide.

They took from the autumn rivers thin, spawning salmon. Their flesh was without fat and almost tasteless until Mattie smoked them over dried alder. Snowshoe hares, in their thick brown hides, Mattie snared and cooked regularly. Canada geese Worcester shot with his fancy new Browning shotgun. And Mattie killed, unerringly with his bow and deadly arrows, ducks and what had become Worcester's favourite-tasting game of all—muskrat.

Mattie snared snowshoe hare—or, as he called them, rabbits. Both men ate them regularly, but here once again Mattie showed Worcester a different way. They were walking back to their camp, along a valley overgrown with alder where they had set rabbit snares two days before. They had caught several rabbits and expected to get a few more before they reached their camp. Although the animals were, for the most part, less than five pounds, a dozen or so of them, along with their other gear, made for a heavy pack.

Mattie stopped without explanation and said, "We lighten our load, maybe."

Shrugging the pack from his broad shoulders and without saying another word, he began cleaning the rabbits. Grabbing one by the head with his left hand, he pressed the entire area below the rabbit's rib cage downward. He repeated this until he was satisfied, and Worcester could see a significant lump in the rabbit's lower abdomen. He now grabbed the animal by its front paws in both hands. Then he flung the rabbit back over his left shoulder while still holding it by its paws. He jerked the rabbit a few times in a rapid motion, then yanked the rabbit back over his shoulder with an amazing speed. When the rabbit reached the full downward swing of Mattie's arms, he stopped it between his legs with a violent whiplash motion, and in the same instant yanked it back.

Worcester stared as the entire contents of the animal's abdomen spewed out onto the ground while the organs inside the rib cage remained intact. Mattie repeated this unique field dressing again and again. When Worcester tried it, and failed repeatedly, he asked Mattie how he made it look so easy.

Mattie said, "Ol' Indian trick." It was a saying Worcester would hear him say many times.

It was the most enjoyable and productive outdoors expedition of Worcester's life. He would never forget the time he spent with Mattie Mitchell. The American clergyman-sportsman shot and killed a black bear that wasn't as big as he thought when they came up to it. Mattie brought the meat back to camp, skinned it out, and that very night got Worcester to try another trapline treat—bear paws. Worcester was a man with the ability to eat anything, or so he thought. He just couldn't bring the bony hands of the bear to his mouth. They looked too much like human hands.

They ate the flesh of fried beaver tail. Mattie told Worcester about the rite among his people to drink the foul-tasting gall of the very first beaver of the season. It ensured a good trapping season, he said. Worcester would not try that either.

They were camped beside a shallow stream late one evening when Mattie told Worcester he was going to catch *elnekat*— eels—for their supper. His people had invented an ingenious tool for this purpose, he said. The *sunkuti* was a pole several feet in length. One end of the pole was cut away to a sharp spear point of a few inches. Whipped securely around the spear and fastened to the pole with thin strips of rawhide were two more wide, wooden, hook-shaped spear points, their edges turned in toward the spear point. When the *sunkuti* was forced down over the eel, the pointed spear pierced its body while the other two points kept its wriggling body in place.

But Mattie had another way of catching them. Worcester, who had come to relish the taste of fried eel—though not as much as Mattie—had seen his guide catch them using his bare hands. He had watched in amazement as the Indian felt under rocks with his long, brown fingers for the snake-like fish. Then Mattie had calmly walked ashore with a struggling, biting eel gripped between his fingers. Mattie's inescapable grip on the slimy fish simply fascinated Worcester. Mattie pointed his long middle finger straight out. The two adjacent fingers were bent toward the palm of his hand. When his probing finger came in contact with the eel, it wrapped around the top of its slippery body and closed like a vice, trapping it against the two fingers below. Worcester tried the grip on dead eels, but he could not nerve himself to probe under rocks for live ones.

Whenever Mattie caught eels, Worcester would watch the Indian clean them. Throwing the eel upon the sand, Mattie would wait as the animal squirmed and twisted. The dry sand stuck to its soft, slimy underbelly slowed its movements. Grabbing a handful of sand, Mattie scrubbed what he called the *skumogan* from its body. Worcester figured it was where the white settlers had gotten the word "scum" from. The rough sand soon made the writhing animal easier to handle. Mattie walked to the nearest tree and cut the skin all the way around, just below the eel's jawline. Holding the eel's head against the trunk with his left hand, he stabbed his knife through its skull with his right, impaling the fish to the tree. The eel never bled a drop. While Worcester watched, Mattie would grip the eel's skin between his fingers and, with one long, steady, continuous pull, relieve the writhing eel of its tough hide.

But on this particular evening, Worcester watched in silence as Mattie fished for eels in a way he had never have thought possible. They had caught a couple of salmon that day. Mattie had kept the strings of ripe eggs from the spawning fish. He called them "the pips."

As Worcester looked on, Mattie tied one of the pink strings of spawn to a long line. He threw the bait into the brook and sat down on his haunches to wait. Worcester had never seen Mattie hunt or fish for anything just for the sport of it. He always did so for food. He wondered why he would he put bait into the water without a hook. Standing over Mattie's shoulder, Worcester soon got his answer. From out of the black depths an eel appeared. It looked to be more than four feet long. Its two small pectoral fins kept its head above the rocky bottom.

The eel's mouth yawed open, and in a slow, almost lazy motion, as if it weren't really hungry but would take the spawn anyway, it swallowed the bait. As it gulped and swallowed the salmon eggs, Mattie paid out the line, giving the eel slack. As the eel swallowed the bait, it kept dragging the line down its gullet along with it. The fish stopped swallowing, turned its head away with a flick of its fins, and headed back to deeper water. Mattie yanked its body around with a strong pull on the line. Standing in a half-crouch, Mattie pulled the line hand over hand.

The startled eel twisted in protest as it was pulled along the bottom. It spun over and over like a giant worm dangling from a trout pole. In seconds, Mattie had pulled the creature up on the shore. He kept pulling the line up out of the eel's stomach. The creature's digestive muscles had such a tight hold on the bait that Mattie lifted the eel off the ground in his efforts.

The salmon spawn, still intact, was half pulled and half vomited from its mouth. The eel fell back to the ground, and Mattie was quick to grip it in his firm "eel grab." He turned to the astonished Worcester and said with a grin, "Anudder ol' Indian trick, Preacher!"

Worcester killed a caribou with one clean shot one early morning. The report from his heavy rifle had not died away before they both saw a long, tawny figure loping away from a pile of rocks nearby.

"Wolf!" hissed Mattie, his eyes following the animal.

As quickly as it had appeared, the wolf faded away again.

Worcester had killed one Newfoundland wolf before. He had also killed a couple of western timber wolves on other hunts in America. But he had never seen a wolf the size of the one that had just vanished into the woods ahead of them. He wanted to go after it, but for the first time since they had been together, Mattie disagreed with him.

"Ver' many wolves not 'ere now. White mans hunt too many. Indian too, maybe. Dat one 'ave fat stomach. She 'ave pups inside, maybe."

They walked back to the pile of rocks where they had seen the wolf and found the animal's lair. They went back to clean the caribou. Mattie left the viscera among the entrails, even though Worcester knew Mattie considered the organs a delicacy.

That night in their camp, miles away from the kill site, they heard the long, howling cry of a wolf several times. Worcester believed the animal sounded like it had a full stomach.

* * * * *

LATE ONE EVENING WHEN THEIR TIME of hunting the wild land was almost done, they wended their tired way back to Mattie's wigwam. Mattie stopped at the edge of the natural clearing where the shelter lay still against a magnificent forest backdrop. He glanced all around when Worcester stepped out of the woods behind him to make his way across. The words "Preacher, stop," came suddenly in a whispered hiss from the Indian's mouth. Taken completely by surprise, Worcester stopped in his tracks and turned to see Mattie concentrating on something.

"Someone bin 'ere! Maybe 'ere still!" he whispered.

"What do you mean? How do you know that?" Worcester whispered back. He looked toward the shelter, half expecting two or more men to rush out of the closed doorway.

They hadn't seen any other human since the day they had left the coast weeks ago. He saw no movement. There was nothing. But something had alerted his Indian guide. He was about to ask what it was when Mattie spoke again, his voice low and even, his lips barely moving.

"Dere—wood junk knocked from pile since we gone." As he spoke his head kept turning around, his eyes hawk-like, searching.

Worcester looked toward the small pile of firewood. He had helped gather the bits and pieces of firewood before they had left the campground. It was Mattie's way to always have a supply of firewood on hand. This was a comforting welcome when returning to camp long after dark, tired and sometimes wet and cold. But Worcester would not have paid attention to one lone piece of firewood resting near the pile. To him it was meaningless. But to his keen-eyed guide it meant a great deal.

Satisfied there was no one around—at least outside of his wigwam—Mattie spoke once more. "Stay 'ere, preacher." It was a rare order from him. And with that the Indian crept silently, half bent, on a diagonal course toward the wigwam's covered doorway. With a fluid stride he reached the doorway in seconds. Bending down to ground level, he lifted the caribou-hide doorway a few inches. Mattie peered inside, fearing the scant light allowed might startle any intruder lurking inside his wilderness home.

He was looking for a set of feet or lower legs, figuring anyone waiting inside would be staring at the door and not the ground. For several minutes he looked all around. He could see no one. He listened intently but could hear nothing.

Standing up, he threw back the hide and stepped inside his dwelling. Worcester arrived behind him tense and breathless, the deep concern of his guide exciting him. He stopped at the edge of the doorway, reluctant to follow Mattie inside. Mattie emerged shortly and without speaking to Worcester walked briskly to the woodpile. He appeared to be angry. Worcester had never seen him angry or the least bit upset.

He walked to where the Indian was standing. Mattie picked up the junk of birch wood, laid it back on the pile, and again glanced all around the campsite. Small patches of well-trod earth were visible in several places around the site, the result of years of human and animal passage. On the edge of the clearing and opposite the way the two men had come was such a spot. It faced a natural lead into the trees and appeared to be a logical way for man or beast to leave the site.

Mattie walked to the spot of bared earth and studied it. Worcester followed him but remained standing. Neither of the men spoke. Worcester had not seen the man in such a state of deep concentration. Finally, Worcester had to speak.

"What is it Mattie?"

Mattie spoke in his normal voice, the tension evidently gone out of him. "Some man 'ere this day. Not long since. One hour, maybe. Not good man."

Worcester stared at the ground. At first he saw nothing, but then he spotted it: the clear partial footprint of a man.

"Maybe it is our track, Mattie."

Mattie looked at Worcester and in a patient voice replied, "Not your track. Too wide, no 'eel. Not my track. Dis man ver' big feet. Dis man running, leave deep track on one side of foot."

Worcester looked again at the man spoor, trying to figure the Indian's reasoning. Mattie was right about one thing. The boot that had made this print would not fit him. Mattie had big feet, but the track was clearly bigger than Mattie's. Worcester looked at his own boots. It wasn't his boot print, either. There was a much deeper print along one side of the track.

Worcester was still puzzled. "How do you know the time he

was here and why do you think he was a bad man? Maybe he was just passing through the campsite."

Just as patiently as before, Mattie spoke as if he were teaching his own son the lore of the woods. "Dis man's weight push small twig into soft groun' without break. Twig not yet swing back. Why good man run from camp?" Mattie shook his head before continuing. "No, I'm sure. Bad man. Good man stop fer tea, we talk trapline way. This man go quick, knock over wood junk. Ver' stupid man."

Worcester knew he had much to learn about the ways of the wild, but he also knew that he had just learned a valuable lesson today. When the signs that were there for him to see with his own eyes had been pointed out to him, he felt inadequate. He had been educated at Columbia University where he received a bachelors degree with the highest of honours. He had excelled at his studies at the University of Leipzig in Germany. But here, in the wilderness where a man had only his wits to get him by, right now he didn't feel like he was a good student.

Back inside the camp, Worcester walked to his bunk and was reaching down for his duffle bag to get his last pair of clean stockings when he noticed his bag was missing.

"Mattie, my duffle is gone! You were right, someone has been here."

Both men looked around for the bag. Mattie was turning to go outside when Worcester called to him. "Wait, Mattie. I did not leave my sleeping robe there in a pile."

In the dingy light of the wigwam, he hadn't noticed it until now. Mattie turned and watched Worcester pull his heavy sleeping blanket away from the floor beside his bunk where it had been thrown in a lump. Underneath the dark blanket gaped the opened mouth of his duffle, its contents spilled and strewn about. Whoever had been here had rifled through Worcester's things and then covered them with his sleeping robe. Mattie's scant belongings were all intact and in place.

Worcester paled. He had left money in a leather pouch in the bottom of his duffle bag. It was nowhere to be seen among the rest of his ransacked belongings.

"My money has been stolen!" he exclaimed in a hoarse, disbelieving cry.

He searched the ground frantically for his money. When he stood from his crawling search, he realized he was alone. Outside again, he found the Indian standing over the lone footprint as before.

"Have you found anything, Mattie?"

But Mattie Mitchell had not been searching for anything. He turned to the man who had become his friend. His dark eyes were angry and fierce to look upon.

"We find nudding. Man come fer money. He leave running with money. When dark come, I get your money back."

And with that, the angry Mi'kmaq walked back inside the wigwam and began building a campfire for their supper. Reaching up to cut a chunk of meat from a haunch of caribou that hung from the slanted ceiling, he noticed the thief had also helped himself to almost half of their meat supply. It only added to Mattie's determination to find the man. And when he did find him, he would pay dearly for stealing from Mattie Mitchell.

Worcester told Mattie his purse had contained $550. It was money to pay his passage back to the States, to pay for provisions, and to pay Mattie for his guiding services. Mattie had never owned that much money in his life and doubted if he had ever seen so much money at one time. But for him it was more than that. His ire would have been the same if the stolen money had amounted to only a few dollars.

He would have gladly shared the piece of venison with any

man. It was the way of the trail. For a man to enter another trapper's camp and take just a little food to help him to his own camp was acceptable. Such a man would leave a sign indicating he had done so. He would never touch or take any personal items belonging to another trapper. The man who had been in their camp had not come by chance. He had come to steal from the American, and while he was here he had decided to help himself to a sizable amount of their food.

As the two men ate their evening meal, their minds were on nothing else but the thief. Worcester agonized about the loss of such a large sum of money, but he could see that Mattie had an overwhelming sense of a great injustice that had been perpetrated against him. It was if something sacred had been taken from him, and it wasn't the meat or the money. He couldn't get past knowing that someone had actually come to this remote valley, had watched them, waited until they left the camp, and then had entered his camp to steal from them.

Dusk came down from the hills and brought with it the dark of night. Small, flickering strands of firelight mingled with the moving man-shadows inside the camp. Outside, the long autumn night had come. Nothing Worcester could say would deter his guide from this venture. He would leave in the darkness. Mattie assured him that he would return by the "grey dawn time" with his money.

"Take my rifle, Mattie," Worcester offered.

He had seen Mattie cast admiring glances over the expensive hunting weapon. Mattie owned an old, well-used, 1871 model Martin Henry rifle, a very heavy, self-cocking, lever action, breech-loading weapon that produced a frightening roar that was matched only by its shoulder-punching recoil.

"Long gun slow me down in dark time. I have good knife."

Mattie placed his right hand on the hilt of the big knife strapped to his side. Worcester knew it was a Bowie knife, which had been given to Mattie by another satisfied American sportsman several years ago.

The nearly foot-long blade was a formidable tool and could become a fearsome weapon at close quarters, especially at night. Designed by Colonel James Bowie in 1830 and forged by James Black, the swedge, or top edge of the knife, was curved away from its deadly point and gleamed with sharpness. Jim Bowie was killed in 1836 at the battle of San Antonio, Texas. The bloody knife in his hand that carried his name had been unable to save him.

CHAPTER 11

PULLING THE STRAPS OF HIS PACK — he went nowhere without it—tight against his shoulders, Mattie stepped out into the chilly night. Worcester followed him through the narrow doorway and caught the barest glimpse of the tall figure crossing the campground as he entered the trace beyond the thief's boot print.

"Have a care, Mattie. God go with you," he said into the night. But he got no answer and stepped back into the warmth of the wigwam, the skin door rustling as it closed behind him.

Standing in the forest gloom only a few steps away from the campground, Mattie waited for his eyes to adjust to the darkness. Campfire light weakened a man's eyesight, but few men could resist staring into the age-old warmth. Knowing his eyes would restore themselves to his keen night vision, he waited and thought about the thief. He knew who it was, but he had not told the preacher man. He heard Worcester give him his blessing.

Maybe he is a priest after all, he thought.

Mattie hated people who stole things and could always tell them at first meeting. They seldom looked a man in the face when talking, but rather averted their eyes, as if fearing others could see into their evil minds. When they stood among a crowd, they frequently cast furtive glances around them, as if anticipating their own nefarious intentions were being planned back upon them. They always boasted of their wilderness feats when in their cups, seated in their musky beer dives, where Mattie was not welcomed nor cared to enter. But when they were in the country, and when night came, they hid inside their hastily built log shanties and opened their doors only a crack to piss out into the long, dark night they so dreaded and feared.

Mattie always avoided their company. Such men carried their bravado well when strutting through the small communities, feeling secure among their own by day and where lamplight glinted from every well-built home at night. They talked down to Mattie at their rare meetings with him, berating the Indian's knowledge at every given opportunity and boasting about their own exploits. Mattie never answered them and only rarely spoke of his wilderness abilities. But away from the security of the villages and deep in the unmarked forested hills, they feared the big woodsman and crossed his trail only by accident: they feared the mystique of the man; they envied his hunting and fishing prowess; they longed to know the secrets of his trapping skills; they feared his ghost-like manner of easy walking. They feared him because they did not know and could not even begin to understand his way.

Thinking about the thief left a burning hatred in Mattie's gut. He wondered if he would kill him when he found him. Away from the campground, he made his way through the dark forest. There was no moon or starlight to help guide his feet along. If he was right about the identity of the thief, he knew the man would not travel far in the dark. However, if the man had run from their camp an hour or so before dark, he could be three or more miles away by now.

There was one thing about the suspected thief that was in Mattie's favour: the man was afraid of the dark. He would not be wandering in the night through a forest he knew little about. This was what Mattie was counting on. He stopped several times and studied the skyline. He knew the shapes of all the mountains and ridges that showed against the sky. It was a mental map to guide his way along. Twice he climbed to high vantage points to spend several minutes searching for a sign.

On one high ridge he stepped up to a large she-spruce tree suitable for climbing. The lower branches hung down and some of them were even embedded in the earth around its huge trunk. Between the bole of the tree and the outer edges of its downward-growing limbs was a circular dry space. Mattie had spent many a comfortable night in such a place. The branches of the big old tree were sturdy and close together. They would make his climb hard, but he grasped a branch anyway and pulled his long body up. The tangly limbs scratched his face and hands as he went.

It took him several minutes of hard climbing to reach more than half the height of the tree. Standing on a limb and clinging onto the tree trunk, he stared all around the country. His fingers were coated with the tree's sticky, scented myrrh. He rubbed them together, trying to remove the gluey substance. For a long while he saw nothing, and for a minute he doubted his reasoning. Then he saw what he was looking for. A glimmer of firelight showed itself in the distance, and once he was sure he saw a few rising flankers!

Mattie smiled in satisfaction. Now he knew he was right. The man he was following had stopped and, in typical white man fashion, had built a huge fire. There was a saying Mattie had for their kind: "Indian light fire for warm. White man light fire for fear."

The thief was one of them. Instead of building a small, low fire and burning dry, seasoned wood that would give off little smoke and no telling sparks, the man had built a bonfire. The Indian had little respect for such a man. In fact, he felt insulted. Did the man think he could just walk into his camp, steal from my "sport," take his food, and expect him not to come after him? This man would regret the day he had stolen from Mattie Mitchell.

Staring at the distant firelight, which flared and sometimes died away, Mattie knew exactly how to get to the man. A valley near him held a small, swiftly running stream that flowed toward a broad, deep river that lay in the thief's path. He had probably left a canoe hidden close to the river for his hurried retreat back to the coast. Mattie had pulled many muskrat from that brook and had walked those riverbanks since he was a young man. He guessed the distance between him and the thief was no more than one easy mile.

Down from the tree and with the direction he was to follow clear in his head, he pulled the pack over his shoulders and headed down over the rim without further thought. There was no need to hurry now. This man wasn't going anywhere until the day came again.

The anger that had possessed him when he left the camp and the preacher had subsided. It was a feeling he was not used to. He was seldom angry at anything. Still, he didn't know how he would react when he confronted the man who had stolen what belonged to Preacher.

* * * * *

HUNCHED DOWN A SAFE DISTANCE AWAY from his blazing fire, the man who had stolen from Mattie Mitchell's camp was terrified. He wasn't a brave man at the best of times and he regretted what he had done. More than that, he regretted where he was and hated and feared the night.

When Mattie had left the hamlet with the rich American to go caribou hunting, he had listened to the talk around town. No one believed the stranger was of the clergy. This American man had money. No minister around here had wealth. Most of them barely got by with the scant donations from their parishioners and their own food gathered from the land and the sea.

The thief had fought against his own inner judgment and his greed won out. The American would certainly take his money with him. He knew that when they reached the caribou barrens, Mattie and his "sport" would be away from their campsite for hours, maybe even days at a time. Looking back on what he had done, the thief smiled. He could hardly believe he had succeeded. He had followed Mattie for two days and as many nights— granted, two nights huddled in the bushes shaking in fear and without a campfire. Only his greed for the American money kept him going. He had run out of food. Luckily, Mattie Mitchell had left some caribou meat behind.

He had hesitated before cutting the bulk of the meat from the hanging caribou quarter. The money—purse and all—belonged to the American, but the meat belonged to Mattie Mitchell. However, his hunger had defeated his caution and his greed directed his hand.

The thief had not even stopped to count the money until just before dark came. He had put several miles behind him, he figured, though he knew he had deviated from his original course. Stumbling upon the bubbling brook more by accident than plan, he was relieved to discover that it was the way back to the river where his leaky canoe waited. He hated the dark. Behind every shadow lurked his fears. The night sounds always startled him.

A roaring fire that demanded constant fuel allayed his fears some and he began to relax. He had pulled it off, done what no one else had ever done. He had stolen from the famed Mattie

Mitchell and was beginning to feel proud of his feat. After all, Mattie was nothing more than a damn Indian. What gave him the right to take rich Americans into the hills anyway? Maybe Mattie would steal the money himself. Everyone knew the Indians were nothing more than lazy, good-for-nothing thieves.

Well, by God, this white man wasn't afraid of Mattie Mitchell. He would be the talk of his drinking buddies. The idea of drinking brought the money to mind. How much was in the fancy leather purse? How much rum would it buy? He wondered if it was American money. Spending foreign currency in the local community would arouse suspicion, for sure, but he knew where it could be done easily enough.

Unable to wait any longer, he yanked the purse from his pocket, squirmed closer to the crackling fire, and pulled the wad of bills free in one excited motion. He gasped when he saw the money. He had not expected it to be so much. The talk around the village was right. The American was rich and clearly not a man of the cloth.

There must be thousands of dollars here!

He shuffled the bills back and forth between his hands, relishing the feel of so much wealth. How he had obtained the money, and the fear of the big Indian, passed. He was far away from the campsite and no one could follow him in the dark, not even Mattie Mitchell. Besides, he figured Mitchell would not be back to his camp that night anyway. The money was his alone. At first light he would be away and down the river to his canoe, and he wouldn't stop until he had paddled along the coast to another community.

The money that filled his hand was all in small denominations. The American had purposely selected low-value bills, rightly figuring that larger ones would be difficult to cash here in these isolated outports. The thief eagerly counted his wondrous booty.

Pulling one bill at a time from his hand, he held it to the light, said its worth out loud—he wasn't good at counting—placed it on the ground between his legs, and fetched another one.

Once, he thought he heard a sound coming from the darkness outside the blazing firelight. He listened for only a second. It was only the echo of his crackling fire, he thought. For a moment his old dread of the night returned, but the lure of the money quickly calmed him and he again returned to his pilfered gains.

By his excited count he had reached $400 and there were many bills left in his hand. He was rich! It had been easy. Why the hell was everyone so scared of Mattie Mitchell anyway? His recent feat against the famed Indian guide gave him a towering sense of bravado. He felt hungry and reached for a piece of the stolen meat warming by the edge of the fire.

* * * * *

THE SOUND THAT HAD ALERTED THE THIEF came from a twig broken under the weight of Mattie's foot. He would not allow it to happen again. He steeled himself when, from his position no more than a few steps away from the man's back, he saw the thief straighten for a moment in alarm.

Scarcely allowing breath, Mattie waited. It didn't take long. The man resumed whatever he was doing and Mattie angled closer. The fire was a big one. It was just as Mattie figured it would be. The thief hunched over as near to it as he dared, and the human form danced in the firelight before Mattie's eyes.

The man was counting money. Mattie could see the piece of meat he had stolen from his camp. The rogue stopped fondling the bills and reached for it. Mattie noticed the man had unusually big feet for his stature.

Once again, Mattie Mitchell felt the terrible urge to kill the man who had stolen from him. He would get his revenge and he knew how. He would cut the man's throat with his deadly knife. Pulling the long Bowie from its leather sheath, he stepped silently toward the man.

The bearded thief reached from his crouched position for another piece of the stolen meat laying by the fire. It wasn't yet hot enough for his liking, but his ravenous appetite would not wait any longer. He selected the biggest piece and leaned back, still in a squatting position, when he was savagely grabbed from behind.

So sudden was the attack that he saw and heard nothing before his breathing was abruptly stopped by a tremendous pressure against his trachea. His head was yanked backwards by the hair so violently that his throat—above the pressure hold that threatened to strangle him—stretched as tightly as new leather on an old drum.

His startled, gagging yell was reduced to a thin, frightened whine. He tried to swallow. His nostrils flared for oxygen. The piece of meat fell from his limp fingers. His knees collapsed underneath him and his lower body sank to the ground in a shocked, trembling bundle of fear. Only his stretched neck and tilted head stayed in place by the force of Mattie Mitchell's powerful arms. The Indian's ferocious grip on the tangled hair on the back of the man's neck caused a burning, tearing pain that made his eyes water and forced an agonized gasp to escape from his clenched jaws.

At first he thought he had been attacked by one of his feared night demons. Then the great crushing pressure was released from his gagging throat. His hair was wrenched more tightly, pulling his head back even farther. His hairy throat stretched farther still, and to Mattie his red, sweat-glazed Adam's apple looked like the bulging breast of a drumming grouse in mating season.

In that same terrible instant, a large brown hand wielding a huge knife appeared in front of his bulging eyes. The razor-sharp swedge of the weapon glinted in the firelight. He tried to turn his neck and his head was thrust farther back. His attacker's knife edge pressed against his unshaven throat.

In absolute terror, the thief realized the knife was on the left side of his throat and lodged against his pulsating carotid artery. There was more to add to his terror. The knife edge was slanted upward so that, if the tearing hold on his scalp was released or if he tried to pull away from the burning pain, he would cut his own throat. In that same fearful moment he knew without seeing who had him in his deadly grip. Through clenched rotten teeth he whined a stammered plea.

"M-Mattie. W-what are you doing 'ere?"

The knife edge burned against his stretched skin. He suddenly felt a wet, sticky substance trickle along his skin.

"N-no, Mattie. Don't, p-please don't kill me! I-I'll give you half the money."

"I take all the money. Den maybe I open your blood vein like caribou!" Mattie's voice rumbled in the night air.

A fire coal suddenly popped. The thief jumped as though he had been shot. The knife pressed harder against his skin.

"Oh my God, Mattie, don't cut me no more! I didn't know 'twas your camp. Take the money and let me go."

"You not only thief, you liar, too. Ever'one know my valley. Maybe I dry shave you before I cut you!"

And with that the burning knife tilted back and travelled up over his skin. His coarse black neck hairs fell free as it went. The scrape of the terrible knife edge was a burst of sound in the man's head. Hot urine soaked through the crotch of his pants and ran down his shaking left leg. The knife finished its upward stroke and slowly dragged back down against the grain, over the exposed raw flesh, until it rested once more against the throbbing blood vein.

"You knows I w-wouldn' steal from you Mattie! 'Twas the 'Merican I took the money from. I'd never take anything of yours, Mattie." The thief finished in a desperate plea for mercy.

"You steal poke from the preacher. You steal from me. You ver' *amassit*—foolish—man. Wot about my smoked deer meat warmin' by your fire?"

Mattie tore the man's head back farther. Now the thief's upturned eyes were looking up at the angry Indian's lean face. It frightened him all the more.

"You c-can't do it, Mattie! I knows you don't kill people," he cried through rotten teeth.

Mattie lowered his face closer to the begging thief and in a voice that hissed loathing said, "No man steal from me before."

The stench emanating from the sweating, unwashed thief reached Mattie's sensitive nose. He turned his head and breathed deeply from the night air. The clean draft of oxygen calmed him. Looking down at the cowardly man between his legs, all thoughts of killing left him.

Somewhere, during his walk through the dark forest, he had felt a shred of grudging respect for the thief who had made his way into the mountains and stolen from him. Now all trace of respect vanished and he released the smelly man from his hold. Bending over the scattered bills, he began stuffing them into his pack.

The thief lay where he had fallen and said nothing as he stared at the Indian. When the last of the American money had disappeared inside his pack, Mattie grabbed the haunch of brown venison and stepped toward the cowering man again.

"You say you not steal from me. Whose deer meat dis?"

The thief saw the flash of anger appear in Mattie's eyes again and found he couldn't speak. He shrank back on his skinny elbows like a beaten pup, his wet crotch plainly visible. He looked down sheepishly.

"You scared the piss out of me, Mattie," he whimpered.

"Smells like more dan dat scared from you," said Mattie, his voice dripping with his utter disgust for the man.

Stepping back to the fire's edge, he hurriedly gathered up each piece of meat, even the piece the thief had tried to eat. He placed them all inside his pack, pulled the leather thongs tight, and swung the bag up on his shoulders. Relieved that Mattie wasn't going to kill him, the man found his voice again.

"Save me some meat, Mattie, please! I've run out of grub and 'tis two days back to the coast fer sure. I'll starve!" he cried.

"Good. You starve. Save me from cutting you next time I see you." The intent in Mattie's voice was clear.

Turning his back on him, Mattie Mitchell strode away from the firelight and vanished into the night forest. He walked carefully back the way he had come until he found the tree he had climbed to spot the campfire. He crawled under the tangled canopy and, with his head on his pack, curled into a fetal position and went to sleep.

* * * * *

THE EASTERN SKY OF MATTIE'S GREY dawn time was smeared with red and pink when he stepped through the door of his wigwam. Kneeling before a small fire Worcester had started in the firepit, Mattie first drew the stolen meat from his pack. Then he upended the bag and watched Worcester's astonished grin as every single bill of his stolen money fluttered to the dirt floor.

Worcester was ashamed to look at his friend. At first he had thought that Mattie himself had taken his money. The big feet, the tall shadow, and Mattie's knowledge of the money had corrupted his better judgment of the man. Worcester could not bring himself to hurt his friend by telling him of his doubt. He wondered for a moment if Mattie would ever forgive him in such a case and somehow knew that he would indeed. But Worcester knew he would never forgive himself. After this day, whenever he looked into the Indian's dark, honest eyes, he was ashamed he had once thought of him as a thief.

Worcester returned to his home in the States before the winter winds came to Newfoundland's shores. He had moored his schooner in a sheltered cove in Bay of Islands before leaving. He returned to his house one day and found his wife in a bit of a quandary. She had received a heavy and roughly constructed wooden box from the north, she said, with his name on it. She had to pay $26 to get it from the postal express. What could it be?

Worcester assured his wife that he hadn't ordered anything from the north, nor was he expecting anything from anywhere else. Upon observing the box, which the postal people had deposited on his front stoop, he read the box was indeed from the northern nation of Newfoundland. Inside he found thirteen tins of canned lobster. The tins were at least a quart in size and weighed, in his estimation, ten pounds each.

Worcester proceeded to open the cans. He found the metal very strong and he had to use his hunting knife to cut through the lid. With a big plate ready on his kitchen table, he prepared for an succulent meal of northern lobster. When he finally pried the lid open, he saw, much to his chagrin, a piece of red flannel. He recognized it immediately as one of Mattie Mitchell's shirts.

Puzzled, he emptied the can over the porcelain plate and was amazed to hear a rattling sound come from a small cloth bag that had dropped out. Inside the bag were sixty glistening pearls! Worcester couldn't believe it. As he searched the rest of the cans, he discovered that Mattie Mitchell had cleverly disguised and shipped to his friend hundreds of pearls that he had laboriously obtained from the cold waters of Newfoundland's western rivers.

* * * * *

MATTIE MITCHELL'S KNOWLEDGE OF THE wild country where he spent almost all of his time was, and still is, the stuff of legend. The northwest part of Newfoundland with its windswept barrens and unusual flat-topped and very high mountains, its heavily forested ridges and deep valleys, and raging rivers that twist through sheer gorges only to plunge suddenly out over vast tracts of open, flat verges, was home to this "chil' of the wilderness." Hunting and trapping, his favourite way to make a living for his wife, Mary Anne Webb, and himself, always took him away to the hills.

Mattie trapped all the way around the magnificent fjord the French had named Bonne Bay. He followed the fur-bearing animals as far as the upper reaches of the Humber River and beyond. He was especially adept at trapping the elusive pine marten, or, as he called it, marten cat. The mammal's rich, lustrous fur always fetched top dollar.

He found the best prices for his furs with the furriers and chandlers who had settled along the shores of Bay St. George. Mattie made his way for many springs over the crusted snow, with his winter's cache of pelts secured to a sled of his own making, down out of the mountains and dark green valleys with the lush, cured furs. The acquired first-hand wisdom of forest life and his intimate knowledge of a largely unknown and very difficult land would serve him in good stead among his own people. As well, they spread his renown beyond his beloved shores to lands that he would never see.

Mattie was a spiritual man, probably without realizing it. Most men who spend long times alone in the wonder of the forest have a spiritual bent, but few will admit to it. There is something about sitting alone under a star-shot sky with the sheen of a full moon casting mysterious shadows everywhere, and the crackle of a small, flickering campfire—the only sound in the world—that causes a man to wonder where he came from, and especially where it is he is going.

CHAPTER 12

MATTIE MITCHELL WAS HUNTER, TRAPPER, lumberjack, and woodsman extraordinaire, as well as an experienced guide and all-seeing prospector. He employed most of his abilities at the same time. His employ of one trade involved and sometimes demanded the skill of the others. Two of his most remarkable skills would put his name on the lips of miners and prospectors and the general population around the Newfoundland island nation. His discovery would become known worldwide. His name would not.

White trappers and explorers, who spent much time along the rivers and many tributaries of the Exploits River in central Newfoundland, marvelled at the immense stands of virgin timber growing on the island. Untouched mature tracts of black spruce and balsam fir, majestic groves of towering pine trees, fields full of glistening, sky-high white birch, and billowing aspens ran the entire length of Newfoundland's long inland valleys.

The timber stands were endless. All of it was untouched, all of it theirs for the taking. Always searching for new opportunities, the industrious trappers and hunters weren't long in talking about the fortunes of timber available all along the Exploits, which was ever ready to transport the waiting wealth to market. News of this bounty soon reached the ears of entrepreneurs and the governing body of the day. The Exploits River would never be serene again.

On a snowy, blustery January 7, 1905, the government of Newfoundland, in partnership with the Anglo-Newfoundland Development Company—or the A.N.D. Company, as it would become known island-wide for the next one hundred years—entered into an agreement. Five months of heated discussion led to its approval, and it passed in the Newfoundland government's legislature on June 13 of the same year. The agreement gave the A.N.D. Company an ironclad lease for ninety-nine years, with a further right for renewal, of an area of 3,000 square miles of land in the forested heart of the Newfoundland island colony. The lease included inland water rights, full mineral as well as quarry rights—an added bonus—falling anywhere within the boundaries of the document. Of course, it included total timber rights.

The modern pulp and paper mill was built on the site of the Grand Falls, twenty miles or so upstream from the fledgling town of Botwood. The deepwater port on the ocean side of the Exploits estuary was needed for the transport of white paper from the mill to world markets. The broad, wooded banks of the Exploits River above the Grand Falls, and the growing town which would bear their name, would yield from its seemingly inexhaustible supply of wood fibre for years to come. Opposition members, who had been against the government's deal in the first place, would never know that it would take nearly one hundred years of pulp and paper production before their fears about signing away all rights to the heartland of the island would become a reality.

* * * * *

ONE OF THE INGREDIENTS REQUIRED FOR the manufacture of pulp into newsprint is sulphur. This non-metallic solid is the thirteenth most common element in the earth's crust. From sulphur comes sodium bisulphate, a derivative essential in the papermaking process.

In 1905, the A.N.D. Company hired Mattie Mitchell to search for sulphur deposits. A significant find of this element would reduce the costs of importing the material to the island. Now Mattie's famous powers of observation would really be put to the test. The company gave him a brief description of what to look for, and after he made preparations for an extended journey, he set off from Grand Falls into the wilderness of central Newfoundland with two fellow A.N.D. Company employees, William F. Canning and Michael S. Sullivan. Mattie Mitchell, who was now in his fifties, was about to start just one of the many chapters of his legend that, sadly, would only be read long after the man was dead.

They headed upstream, keeping to the shorelines of the Exploits River. They searched the many ponds and lakes that flowed into the big river valley on their way. The men knew their best chance at finding a sulphur deposit lay where the water had caused erosion. Mattie was their leader. He just seemed to have a sixth sense for direction. The men would talk by their night fire and decide on the next day's traverse, and in the morning Mattie would lead off toward the agreed-upon site without compass or map.

Mattie seldom followed his people's rule of travel these days. Though he knew very well the "Red Indian this way, Mi'kmaq this way" mantra, and still harboured some misgivings, he went into the forbidden areas anyway when he crossed the invisible divide. However, he always paused before entering valleys or before crossing rivers where he knew the Red Indians had been. Canning and Sullivan simply thought Mattie was studying the lay of the land and choosing the best route. He appeared to tread lightly as they approached the eastern end of Red Indian Lake. Mattie called it "the Red Pond." Mattie didn't voice his concerns aloud to his companions, nor did he mention the great sadness that always shuddered through his body when he knew they had crossed an old trace of the Beothuk's passing. The signs were never fresh, only faded and weathered, until only their spirit remained, felt only by those who believed in such things.

When the three men reached the place where the wide mouth of the Exploits sucked great volumes of water away from Red Indian Lake, they crossed over the narrow inlet at the lake's east end by boat and journeyed west along its northern shore. As they searched all along that shore and walked upstream a fair distance to explore every one of the brooks and streams that poured into the lake, Mattie's companions always felt as though their Indian guide was impatient to continue travelling.

When they reached the mouth of Sandy River, later to be named the Buchans River, Mattie seemed to be content and led his small party steadily upstream. His step seemed to be more earnest than usual as they journeyed upriver.

The British had left their mark at Red Pond in 1811, nearly one hundred years before. The Buchans River got its name from a Royal Navy lieutenant, David Buchan, who was one of the few Englishmen who had shown some concern for the plight of the few remaining native Beothuk Indians. In a vain effort to communicate and establish relations with the elusive Beothuk, he had headed an expedition to the frozen shores of this Red Indian Lake.

In the winter of 1811, the ambitious lieutenant indeed made contact with the Indians, and was so confident he would be accepted into their trust that he left two of his men to spend the night in the Beothuk camp. Before noon the following day, they saw red blotches on the white snow long before they reached the site. His two men had been beheaded, but not before a brutal fight for their lives. The campground, and even the frozen lake nearby, was spattered with the blood of his two soldiers. The Beothuk had long since disappeared into the silent forest. Buchan was devastated, as much for his failed contact with the Indians as for the loss of his men.

Buchan returned to the frozen Red Indian Lake again in 1820. This time he brought with him the body of a Beothuk woman her people called Demasduit. The whites called her Mary March, after the Blessed Virgin, Mary, and for the month in which she was captured by the whites. Demasduit had died in captivity, from the white man's terrible lung disease, tuberculosis. Buchan left Demasduit's body in a hastily built teepee near the river that would eventually bear his name and retreated back to his schooner in the Bay of Exploits.

* * * * *

MATTIE LOVED HIS "CUPPA TEA." He was always the one who chose the spot for their mug-up. The place he chose to boil the kettle on the banks of Sandy River on this expedition would change the history of Newfoundland forever.

On this day he decided to lunch and boil up on a large outcrop that jutted out of the riverbank and which disappeared into the rushing water. He usually looked around some before deciding on a place for their meals. This time he didn't take any time making that decision. He simply walked below the overhanging rock, removed his pack, and announced that this was where they would rest and make tea.

The outcrop upon which he had started a fire close to the river had a reddish brown stain running through it. In some places it was grey, and in other places a yellowish green stain ran out of the cliff. All three men recognized that this geological formation contained some kind of unusual rock. As it turned out, the discovery didn't contain sulphur, but sulphides. Mattie led the others to two more outcrops of the same material in the same area.

They spent two days carefully choosing the best rock samples to take back with them. During all this time Mattie didn't appear surprised or even excited. It was as if he had known where to find this strange rock. The samples they took back were a thousand times more valuable than sulphur. What Mattie Mitchell had led the men to was the biggest sulphide-based metal deposit in the world. It contained copper, lead, zinc, gold, and silver.

It would take five more years before the first motor-driven boat would take 1,000 tons of samples of the ore across Red Indian Lake to the railhead. From the railcar it was loaded on board a ship at the new port of Botwood, and from there shipped to Sweden for testing. The A.N.D. Company learned that Mattie's find was extremely valuable. However, the technology to separate the various minerals was not known.

The flotation process needed to separate them was not perfected until 1925, when the American Smelting and Refining Company (ASARCO), at its metallurgical lab in Flat River, Missouri, finally solved the problem. Two years more passed, and on May 19, 1927, ten men arrived at the site that would bear the name Buchans and started the groundwork for a world-class mine.

Over its lifespan the Buchans mine would yield out of its depths 16.2 million tons of some of the richest high-grade ore on the planet, with a combined value of US $3.6 billion. In 1905, in thanks for his discovery, Mattie Mitchell received his wage of $18 per month, plus a bonus of one barrel of flour for his discovery. The barrel of flour was worth $2.50.

CHAPTER 13

THREE YEARS LATER, NOW SIXTY-FOUR years old and still working for the A.N.D. Company, Mattie Mitchell started out on yet another adventure that would again make an amazing first for Canada, and of course for the island of Newfoundland.

This part of Mattie's story really begins with yet another European's influence on the island as well as Labrador. It started with his direct involvement with a northern race of native people, the Innu—formally called Montagnais—as well as the Inuit, or Eskimo people. Unlike many on the long list of Europeans who had exploited the native population all around the coasts, Grenfell's mission was one of mercy.

Dr. Wilfred Thomason Grenfell was an Englishman born on February 28, 1865, in Parkgate, a small town in the north of England. He attended medical school in London, where he received his degree. Grenfell was a very spiritual man, a devout Christian who would live and practice his beliefs his whole life. He became a member of the Royal National Mission to Deep Sea Fishermen, an organization involved in the welfare of fishermen not only in Britain, but throughout the British Commonwealth and its colonies.

As a member of this group, Dr. Grenfell was sent to

Newfoundland in 1892. His charge was to find out the living conditions of the fishermen and their families along the northern coast of the island of Newfoundland and on the north coast of Labrador. What the good doctor saw as he travelled astounded him. What affected the man most of all were the terrible living conditions of the native peoples as well as many of the white people struggling for existence, both on the tip of the island and along the coast of Labrador.

The main, overriding challenge among their many problems was a constant supply of winter food. The huge floes of spring ice moving south along the Labrador coast always brought with them millions of harp seals. It was a bounty from the sea and rich in protein. They caught codfish and stored them from summer until late fall, but it was never enough.

The long, terrible winters were the bane of Grenfell's medical skills. The malnourished were the first to succumb to disease. Grenfell saw more than he could deal with. The distance he had to cover in order to bring sound medical advice and attention to these coastal people was considerable. The doctor could hardly believe that the breadth of this land was so sparsely populated yet could swallow whole the land of his birth.

Always, wherever he travelled, he preached to what he so lovingly called "my people" the need for good hygiene and proper food. He determined the people would benefit immensely from a constant supply of meat, one for which they would not have to continuously hunt over long and insurmountable distances. The mainstay of fresh meat in this area were the huge caribou herds. One of them, the George River herd in Labrador, was the largest migrating caribou herd in the world. The other, smaller herd on the island nation was a species of caribou native to the island of Newfoundland and had the distinction of being the most southerly herd of woodland caribou anywhere in the world.

However, they were hunted in excess and the small herds on the Northern Peninsula dwindled.

Harp seals were readily available along the coast when the huge ice floes brought the breeding mammals along the coasts of Labrador and Newfoundland annually. But this was only a springtime event and far from sustainable. Grenfell thought he had the answer to at least some of the problem. He would bring in reindeer from Scandinavia.

The deer of Lapland had been domesticated in that part of the world for centuries. The reindeer were a tough northern breed of animal. They were in fact caribou of a different name in northern Europe. *Qalipu* is their North American Mi'kmaq name, one of the few native names the Europeans kept, although they changed the spelling and pronunciation to "caribou."

Grenfell thought about taming the native caribou, but wisely decided that the time needed to bring the animals to a controlled domestic state, as had been done with the reindeer in Europe, would take generations. The reindeer from northern Europe could be free-ranged and corralled here and raised for slaughter, much like the Canadian prairie cattle herds. As an added nutritional bonus, the reindeer could be milked.

Grenfell knew the Laplanders drank the milk from their herded animals. He also knew the milk from the reindeer contained four times as much butterfat as the milk from dairy cows. Fresh milk was non-existent along these northern shores. Grenfell had brought midwives with him from England who related to him that the only source of milk found in homes where they provided their badly needed services was in the breasts of birthing mothers.

A constant supply of calcium would also go a long way in controlling the crippling disease of rickets prevalent among Newfoundlanders and Labradorians. Even the sailor's disease called scurvy was prevalent, as well as anemia, scrofula, and the constant presence of tuberculosis, diseases whose presence owed largely to lack of proper nutrition.

Dr. Grenfell was sure his idea would work. He knew that reindeer had been "ranched" successfully in Alaska, and he could see no reason why it wouldn't work here as well.

Money was raised and the great venture began. Grenfell chose for his experiment the reindeer from Lapland, that area of northern Europe bordering on the Arctic Ocean that includes parts of Norway, Sweden, Finland, as well as the Kola Peninsula of Russia. The climate and the terrain were much the same as those in northern Newfoundland and southern Labrador. Grenfell studied long and hard before making the final decision. The land of the reindeer had forests of black spruce and fir and pine, along with great stands of white birch. The animals fed and grew in abundance on huge expanses of tundra-like land much the same as that of this island colony.

There would be no need to buy food for the reindeer. It had to work. Grenfell was excited, convinced. "The food for them is inexhaustible, the land unappropriated," he stated.

This extraordinary man, whose mind was never at rest and who always acted on his every thought, and who constantly had the welfare of the northern people foremost in all of his endeavours, was about to begin yet another of his many ventures. Without knowing it, his venture would add an amazing, closing chapter to the story of Mattie Mitchell.

Grenfell would go down in grateful history as one Englishman who had not exploited this "new world" at all, but one who had seen a great void and had willingly devoted his entire life to alleviating that terrible need. He was a missionary and confessor, a doctor, a surgeon; a policeman, magistrate, and judge; a teacher and compassionate healer; a businessman, entrepreneur, adventurer, and scientist. He was an eager pioneer and tireless explorer, sailor, and cartographer; engineer and sawmiller; a builder and craftsman. He was dearly loved and a friend to all.

News of the unusual proposed import reached the company officials at the pulp and paper mill in Grand Falls. Always looking for a way to cut the high costs of getting logs to their mill, they saw in Grenfell's project what could very well be a partial solution to some of their wood-hauling costs. The reindeer were used not only as a source of meat in Lapland but also as draft animals. The mill owners did some investigating of their own. They were very pleased with the results.

One reindeer could pull as much as 450 pounds as far as forty miles in one day. It could pull a sled with two heavy men riding on it at eighteen miles an hour. This was very encouraging to company officials always looking for ways to cut log-harvesting costs. An added feature, and the most cost effective of all, was that the animals could eat from the surrounding forests. No more would costly hay and oats dig into their profits.

They learned that one square mile of barrens with a healthy growth of caribou moss could support thirty reindeer forever. Not only that, they could also dine on the yellowish green moss hanging from so many of the spruce trees—which the loggers called maw dow—the company was harvesting. Their research also revealed that the animals loved the tips of birches, alders, and grasses. The four-chambered stomachs of the cud-chewing ruminates could digest almost all available food. And all of it free.

If the venture didn't work out, they could always kill the reindeer and use the meat to feed their loggers. The company couldn't lose. The company learned that the Laplanders drank the reindeer milk, but this was not important to them. Their loggers didn't drink milk anyway.

The Anglo-Newfoundland Development Company Limited

contacted Dr. Grenfell and asked him to add fifty extra animals to his order to be landed at their dock in the seaport town of Lewisporte. Providing, of course, the company could have the animals delivered at draft horse prices or better. Grenfell agreed, and the great forced reindeer migration began.

Dr. Grenfell paid an initial price of $8.50 for each of the reindeer on the hoof in Lapland. The total costs of freight and for feeding the animals on their transatlantic crossing to St. Anthony came to $51.49. The owners of the steamship *Anita* charged $1,750 for the winter cruise, along with an additional $0.50 per reindeer head to be given to the captain of their vessel, providing the deer reached Newfoundland in good health.

Sami herders drove the 300 reindeer across much of Lapland to the Alten Fjord on the north coast. The herdsmen had been hired not only to deliver the animals to the coast, but to accompany them across the ocean to Newfoundland. The Sami herders also brought with them their herd dogs and insisted on taking their families. They would not leave without them.

Although the Alten Fjord sat well within the Arctic Circle, December of 1907 brought little snow. Getting the deer to the ship wasn't a problem, but hauling the more than 500 sledloads of moss needed to feed them on their North Atlantic voyage slowed their progress considerably. On December 30, with all 300 reindeer safely aboard the SS *Anita*, each one of them stowed in its own hastily built "berth," the steamship gathered way and headed into the Arctic darkness, down the long, freezing fjord, and to the open North Atlantic ocean.

For the next twenty days, over half of them bringing violent storms, the *Anita* sailed westward. Most of the Laplanders became severely seasick. The reindeer, with their antlers cut to prevent injury during the crossing, were constantly tossed about, but their narrow stalls protected them. The human vertigo condition seemed to have no effect on them at all. The ruminates took each daily serving of moss in one end and, after passing it through all four of their stomach chambers, deposited it again, minus all nutrients, in stinking, braided black buttons from the other end. Before the *Anita* was hull down in the North Sea, her bilge had taken on a distinctive earthy odour.

On the twenty-first day at sea, January 20, 1908, the *Anita* hove to off the rugged entrance to St. Anthony, only to discover the harbour was completely frozen over. The ship sailed eight miles farther south along the winter coast to the slob ice off Cremaillere Bay.

Now began a peculiar sight for the people watching from shore. The ship embedded itself into the pounded ice edge as far as the captain dared and began discharging its cargo. Two hundred and fifty of the reindeer walked up and out of the ship's hold onto shaky wooden ramps and down onto what appeared to be a frozen white bay. They were reportedly in "splendid" condition and, looking alert and seemingly curious, they started to walk ashore.

However, the porous slob ice could not bear up to the weight of the reindeer and they frequently broke through into the icy water. In the confusion, many of them swam back to the open sea. Later they were found miles from land and still swimming in a northeasterly direction, toward northern Europe! Farther in from the edge, the ice was sound and many of the reindeer headed for shore, where they immediately began browsing the tops of green scrub spruce trees that rose out of the deep snow.

A few locals observed that at least two of the reindeer appeared to have symptoms resembling human seasickness. They seemed to sway a bit as they walked, but this was likely the result of adjusting their four sea legs all at one time. They paused with heads down, their long necks outstretched, their throat muscles twitching but discharging nothing. However, their weird, four-legged sailor's gait soon left them and, with the snarling dogs at their heels carrying out the commands of their human masters, they followed the rest of the herd to the foreign shoreline.

The Lapland herders, resplendent in their colourful deer hides, walked behind the curious reindeer. The herders had with them several dogs trained in the art of keeping the fleet-footed deer together. Cremaillere, with its half a dozen or so small, unpainted houses, had more than three dozen sled dogs, all of them wanting a piece of the new "foreign" dogs out on the harbour ice.

The herdsmen, who had endured and survived their first North Atlantic crossing in the dead of winter, were Sami, an indigenous people from Lapland who had domesticated the deer of their homeland for hundreds of years. They couldn't speak a word of English. Fortunately, the ever-thoughtful Dr. Grenfell had provided a person who could manage enough of the Scandinavian tongue to act as translator. By the time darkness had set in, the cargo intended for the Grenfell herd, complete with herders, their families, and their dogs, were safely ashore.

Fifty reindeer remained aboard the ship to be transported farther south along the northeast coast of Newfoundland, where they would be off-loaded at the town of Lewisporte, Notre Dame Bay, at the A.N.D. Company's dock. One Sami family and four of their herd dogs remained aboard the *Anita* to accompany the fifty reindeer to their final destination. Just as the ship was building up steam to leave, word came from Grenfell that Notre Dame Bay was frozen solid and there would be no entry from the sea. So the remaining fifty reindeer were off-loaded with the others.

The fifty reindeer now belonging to the A.N.D. Company—forty of them pregnant females—were slated for work as log-hauling draft animals at the company depot in Millertown on the shores of Red Indian Lake, and if they couldn't get at least part of the way there by sea, then by God they would walk all the way there by land.

There was no other way. But who would take on such a task? Not only that, who knew the way through the treacherous, winter-stormy Long Range Mountains? There was only one man who had the knowledge and the ability to carry this daunting feat through. Fortunately for Hugh Cole, the Anglo-Newfoundland Development's manager, such a man was already in the employ of the company, the sixty-four-year-old Mi'kmaq Mattie Mitchell.

Hugh Wilding Cole was a young Englishman who had come to work for the A.N.D. Company just two years before and had proven himself to be a valuable asset to the company. He was fearless and strong, both in muscle and will. Cole had arrived in St. Anthony on Christmas morning, 1907, in preparation for the reindeer arrival.

He had brought with him translator Morris Sundine, a man whose native tongue was Swedish. Cole had no way of knowing when the ship would arrive, so, leaving Sundine to remain in St. Anthony, he left again by the coastal boat *Prospero* under the command of fifty-three-year-old Abram Kean. The trip south on the *Prospero* was not a good one. The boat encountered winter storms almost day and night. The ship *Prospero*, named for Shakespeare's character in *The Tempest*, earned its name on this winter's voyage. The ship finally arrived in the outport of Little Bay in Notre Dame Bay, where Hugh Cole hired a dog team and its musher and finally made it to company headquarters in Grand Falls.

The company's decision was to bring the reindeer—for which they had paid good money—to Millertown as planned. Cole was instructed to leave as soon as possible for Norris Point, Bonne Bay, and pick up Mattie Mitchell, who would guide them north to St. Anthony and bring the reindeer back with him overland.

Cole took Tom Greening, a company foreman and experienced woodsman, and both men travelled by train as far as Deer Lake, which was as far north as they could get by rail. Cole's freight car contained a dogsled, five hauling dogs, some camping gear, and enough food for a week or so.

They arrived in Deer Lake at 9:30 p.m. on a cold Saturday night, January 25, 1908. By the time they were ready to leave Deer Lake on January 27, three feet of snow covered the frozen ground. By 3:30 p.m. the temperature had risen and it rained, making the going very difficult. By the time they had stitched together their bed of fir boughs, the rain stopped, the clouds shifted, and they slept fitfully under a mantle of bright stars. They had travelled only four miles northwest from Deer Lake.

The rain began again sometime before dawn and it continued until midday. With the heavy rain and mild weather, travel was impossible. In true Newfoundland style, the temperature dropped drastically that night, the skies cleared, and Cole and Greening broke camp again. On January 29 they travelled a full twenty miles. They reached Bonne Bay at 3:00 p.m. on Thursday, January 30.

They crossed from the bottom of the long eastern arm of the bay to the small village of Norris Point by boat. They arrived late in the cold winter afternoon and Cole knocked on Mattie Mitchell's door. A shy, black-haired, and very pretty woman answered after his second knock. Opening the door only halfway, she told them her husband wasn't at home. Cole told her who he was and introduced Tom Greening. Mary Anne relaxed when she learned they were from the A.N.D. Company. She wasn't used to having strange white men knock on her door late in the evening.

Mattie's wife told the two men that she expected her husband home before nightfall, but then cautioned timidly, "My man always bring dark on 'is shoulder."

Long after the dark had come, Mattie Mitchell came crunching along the snow-packed gravel road to his door and shortly met with Cole and Greening. He agreed to lead them on the trek to St. Anthony without question. When Cole asked him if he would consider taking on the task of guiding a herd of fifty reindeer from St. Anthony to Millertown, Mattie asked him what reindeer were.

Cole told him they were really caribou but with a different name. He told him where the animals had come from and explained his company's experiment and the need to get the animals to their depot in Millertown. Mattie considered for a moment and then agreed to lead them.

Cole knew that Mattie had guided the geographer H.C. Thompson up over the Great Northern Peninsula in 1904 on an extensive mapping expedition for the Newfoundland government. He asked Mattie if he had a copy of one of the maps that Thompson had compiled. Mattie told him he didn't have one of the paper maps but that he had the route in his head.

Another winter storm blew in from the sea and snow lashed with northwest winds, stranding them in Norris Point until February 3, when they finally left for St. Anthony. They reached Lobster Cove just north of Rocky Harbour that night.

And then, quite suddenly, Mattie Mitchell became ill. Red blotches appeared on his face and legs and gave him considerable pain accompanied by fever. Mattie had erysipelas.

The expedition made it as far as Gulls Marsh the next day, when Mattie's resistance and great strength gave out. They didn't make a decent camp and huddled around their campfire in misery.

They stayed there for two days until Mattie appeared to have improved. The big Indian refused to let the others carry or let the dogs haul his load. On the late evening of February 7, when they walked into the tiny settlement Parson's Pond with snow drifting all around them, he collapsed. His illness had overtaken him. They waited for three days, without any medicine, for their guide to heal.

The morning of February 11 dawned cold and sunny, and still the water of the nearby Gulf of St. Lawrence was "stark calm." Mattie told Cole his sickness had passed and that he was ready for the trail again. They crossed the mouth of the river at Parson's Pond using a local fisherman's boat and followed a good, snow-packed trail until they reached Portland Creek by dusk of that day. That night the three men set up their tent and made a good camp.

Before leaving the next day, Cole bought a new, harness-broken sled dog, and two hours after dark that night they mushed into River of Ponds. They had made twenty-six hard miles that day. The next day Greening became ill with "la grippe" and slowed them to walking only six miles, after which they made camp at Trappers Cove on February 13, just south of the entrance to Hawke's Bay.

They crossed the end of that frozen bay the next day and prepared to cross over from the west side of the Northern Peninsula to the east side. Here in Hawke's Bay, Mattie was assisted by William Uland, who knew of a trail that would take them across. Following his advice, the team made the journey across the peninsula.

They encountered another mild day that turned cold at night, forming a thin crust on the snow which made for hard going. However, on Monday, February 18, after making their way twenty-four miles down the Cloudy Brook Valley, they made it to Dr. Grenfell's sawmill. After walking across the ice in Hare Bay on February 20, they took shelter from a blizzard in an abandoned home in Island Bight. From there they pressed on until they finally made it to St. Anthony on Friday, February 21, with Mattie Mitchell leading the way.

The men made preparations over the next several days for the trip south. They obtained heavy tents complete with small funnel holes in their slanted roofs, along with small portable wood-burning stoves and sleeping robes, which they hoped would keep them warm in the winter nights. Finally, they bought food for all of the party as well as for the dogs.

Winter gales with snow, mild days with rain and dense fog, and temperatures dropping to five degrees below zero hampered their goal of cutting the A.N.D. Company reindeer from the rest of Grenfell's herd. At long last, on March 4, the herd and the humans all came together at Locks Cove. The reindeer trek with the Mi'kmaq Mattie Mitchell walking proudly in point position, stood ready to add another historical, adventurous first to the varied pages of Newfoundland lore.

Cole had with him a Lapland herder, sixty-five-year-old Aslic Sombie, and his wife of thirty-six years, their thirty-year-old son, Pere, and their daughter Maretta, who was thirty-two and could neither speak nor hear. Cole's interpreter, Morris Sundine, Thomas Greening, and Mattie Mitchell made up the eight people who would do what had never been done before.

The original plan was to follow the winter sea ice as far as possible, maybe to the bottom of White Bay, and from there cut overland to Millertown. However, by this late date the huge Arctic ice floes had shifted south in their ceaseless spring migration. Cape Bauld had been dividing and checking the mighty white floes for weeks, sending massive sheets of ice south in swiftly moving streams along the land toward the warm waters of the Gulf of St. Lawrence. The island of Newfoundland now had a white bridge to the mainland of Canada.

On the Atlantic side of the Great Northern Peninsula, as far as the eye could see, the shifting icefields had come and filled every cove and bay as they poured along by the land and silenced the surrounding sea. Great blue swatches of open water could be seen everywhere when the men viewed the sea from high points of land. These open areas of water would close and open without warning as the wind shifted or as the tide ebbed and flowed. A decision was reached to follow the shore ice as far as possible to the western end, and possibly the southern end, of Hare Bay, and then abandon the ocean crossing in favour of the longer but much safer route overland.

Somewhere in the mysterious time of pre-dawn, a leviathan had reached up and leaned in from the changing sea behind it to take a huge, jagged bite out of the Northern Peninsula, almost severing its defenceless head. This five-mile-wide stretch of water at the mouth of Hare Bay, penetrating eighteen miles inland, was where the reindeer drive really began.

The exposed vertebrae along the spine of Newfoundland's Great Northern Peninsula is not for the timid or the faint of heart on the warmest of summer days. With the grip of late winter still firm upon the land, the very idea of travelling, on foot, the entire length of that winter-bound peninsula—let alone nursing along a herd of semi-wild animals—seemed ludicrous. Many of the local trappers who knew the immediate area better than Mattie Mitchell doubted that it could be done. Though Hugh Cole figured the route would be a challenge for anyone—especially after the trip up from Deer Lake—he had such dependence in Mitchell's wilderness lore and incredible sense of direction that he entrusted him with the task of guiding his party the entire unmapped route.

With his easygoing, carefree manner, Mattie didn't see the trip as anything more than a prolonged walk "on the country."

CHAPTER 14

HOWEVER, THE EASY, TIME-SAVING way across the frozen Hare Bay was not possible. Due to the recent rain and subsequent freezing, the bay had turned into a black, icy sheet. The reindeer would not be able to keep their footing on such a slippery surface, so Cole made the decision to walk around the bay, increasing their trek by forty miles.

Leaving the sea behind them, the group set out for the distant Long Range Mountains, the northernmost link of the huge Appalachian chain that began far south on the North American continent. Mattie Mitchell, with his tireless, long-legged stride, was the vanguard of the group. He walked on leather-tied snowshoes of his own design and making.

The small party of nomad-like travellers were a sight to behold, with an Indian stepping boldly out in front, constantly breaking trail through the deep, snow-clogged valleys and sparse scrublands and deep forests alike. Following behind him came the smooth-stepping deer, their flaring black nostrils forcing grey, plumed mists into the frigid air that hung like wreaths above them as they moved along. Next came the endlessly barking dogs, running along the sides and sometimes behind the reindeer in response to their foreign master's yelling. And then came the Sami herder and his family, all dressed resplendently from head to feet in the skins of the animals they had come to herd. Inside their nearly knee-high reindeer skin boots, their feet were wrapped in dried grasses.

Bringing up the rear of the caravan came the sled dogs, their muscles straining as they pulled the load, some of them with their ribs showing. All had pink tongues bouncing out the sides of their toothy jaws as they plodded along a snow trail broken by the snorting reindeers' broad hooves.

To stay ahead of the high-stepping reindeer was impossible, even for Mattie, whose stride was long. At the very start of the journey, the always inventive Mi'kmaq would start off ten or so minutes before the others. This allowed him time to decide on the best trail direction, as well as the safest routes to stay on track, before the reindeer caught up with him. Mattie always feared the animals would step on the backs of his snowshoes if they came too close, even though the lead deer always stopped a few feet behind him as it snorted impatiently.

As the trip wore on, the reindeer would follow Mattie Mitchell's every twist and turn and stop whenever he stopped. Their herder and his yapping dogs could move them from behind, but the reindeer would follow no one but the Indian.

On March 7, by the time the expedition camped for the night near Main Brook Pond, the Laplander Pere Sombie was suffering badly from snow blindness. Mattie made a band from the soft inner bark of a birch tree, cut narrow slits for the eyes, and got the man to tie it around his head. It worked so well the Sami man kept it around his head day and night until the bark finally broke.

They found out very early about the herding instinct of the reindeer. At every opportunity, the animals would head back toward St. Anthony. At night the party had no choice but to keep a constant watch over them, in four-hour shifts.

Cole also discovered, on their very first day on the trail, a custom of the Laplanders that caused him a great deal of consternation. The Lap woman and her daughter both rode in a sled called a *pulka* which their labouring dogs pulled. The *pulkas* had arrived with the Lap herders and were intended to be used for the trip. They were shaped like barrel staves, no more than a foot high, two feet wide, and less than six feet long. The sleds proved to be totally useless. They worked well in the cold, dry Arctic climate of Lapland, but here on the coast of the ever-changing Atlantic climate, the soft, damp snow kept piling up in front of the sled until the dogs could not pull them.

As soon as he could make arrangements, Cole replaced them with the Newfoundland komatik. The two women then rode in the komatiks and, despite further arguments from Cole, refused to walk. It was their custom, they told him, and when Cole shouted his protest, they yelled words back at him that his translator, Sundine, could not understand. Cole was sure they were cursing at him.

They were crossing a large pond on Monday, March 9, when they were surprised to see two dog teams approaching them. Drs. Little and Stewart were returning to St. Anthony from Englee, where they had been attending to several patients.

The doctors were amazed at the sight of the reindeer walking behind the tall Indian. They talked for a while about the trail ahead and the snow that never seemed to end. The doctors wished Hugh Cole every success with his venture. With a yell to their restless dogs and running behind their komatiks, the two men mushed away to the north. The misshapen pond where they met would take Cole's name on maps of Newfoundland.

They walked out to the frozen northwest arm of Canada Bay on March 10 after walking fourteen miles in the teeth of yet another winter storm. The temperature was well below zero, visibility was poor, and everyone—except the bundled women—was tired.

Cole decided to leave for the outport community of Englee to buy supplies. In spite of the late hour and the poor weather, they started out, with Mattie in the lead. They took no dog team or sled. It was Cole's intention to buy a sled as well as a small dog team at Englee to haul the grub back.

Along the way they found several blazed trees and, in a few places where the snow had swept clean, the faint traces of the doctors' trail. They arrived back in Canada Bay the next day. The snow had stopped but the high winds continued, and with it severe drifting, too bad for further travelling. Cole ordered Aslic Sombie to put an ox—a gelded stag—in harness and break it for pulling while they waited for the wind to abate.

With the wind finally easing a bit, they left Canada Bay the next morning and made their way southwest over the high hills to Cloudy Brook and camped for the night. They made twelve hard miles on Friday, March 13, after chopping a rough trail through the dense growth along the river. It had rafted up with broken ice, making it impossible to cross.

One of the local dogs that Cole had bought in Englee harassed the reindeer at every opportunity. Cole had punished the dog for its behaviour once, but, given the chance, the dog always approached the deer with ferocious barks and snarling bites. While they were getting the deer through the narrow trail they had cut, the dog chewed free of its leather harness and slunk away toward the lead animals.

Mattie heard the dog barking but paid it no heed. The Lap dogs were always barking. Then he heard an unusually vicious, wolf-like snarl coming from behind him. When he turned, the new dog had the lead stag—which had been quietly following Mattie—in a ferocious grip by the hind leg that drew blood.

With one long step, Mattie reached the animals. Without breaking his stride, he directed a kick at the dog. The rounded front of his snowshoe lashed soundly against several of the dog's taut ribs and it ran away yapping and crying in pain.

The frightened lead deer bolted into the woods, snow flying from its legs as it ran. Mattie followed it for a while and then came back to report the attack to Cole, who found the dog cowering behind one of the loaded komatiks. He had intended to beat the dog, but seeing that Mattie's big foot had inflicted punishment enough, he tied it in place with the other dogs using a heavy rope. It snowed again that night, a blinding, wind-hurled snow that cut into a man's eyes if he looked into it. When the morning came the crippled stag had returned . . . but thirty of the other reindeer had disappeared!

* * * * *

MATTIE HELPED THE SAMI HERDER, who had seen dogs inflict wounds on reindeer many times before, make up a kind of poultice for the wounded stag. The animal's left hind leg between the pastern and the knee was badly torn. Without speaking and using a practical sign language, the two indigenous men used what their people had always used, natural medicine. They found spruce frankum and heated it to a gluey paste. The men chopped through the rough outside bark of a young tamarack tree and scraped off handfuls of the pink, stringy inner bark, which the Sami pounded into a pulp.

They blended the spruce resin and the tamarack paste together, and applied the compound to the reindeer's leg, holding the salve in place with a soft bandage of birch bark. When the Sami knelt to administer aid to the deer he was honour bound to protect, the Mi'kmaq Indian, who had killed hundreds of caribou, stood at the animal's neck and whispered into its twitching ear a language that only he and the deer understood. The deer shivered all over but didn't once move its injured leg.

Cole had a terrible row with Aslic, who wanted to stay until the other reindeer returned, even if it took as long as a week. Cole absolutely refused. He believed the deer would return on their own. Besides, the weather was too bad for searching, and added to that fact was the tracking problem. There were caribou in the area, and they would be wasting their time tracking reindeer that could very well *be* caribou. As soon as the weather permitted, they would move on.

Late at night on Tuesday, March 17, the wind finally blew itself out. In the morning they went looking for the reindeer. Cole and Sundine returned to camp with nothing, but Mattie, who had Greening and Pere with him, came back with ten of the roving animals. Mattie had found them feeding by a brook five miles away. During the day, Mattie found more of the herd. By mid-afternoon the remainder had returned on their own.

The evening was clear and bright, so they decided they would move out over the barren hills ahead of them. They kept moving until several hours after dark, when they entered the woods again. Here they stopped for the night. The men smoked their pipes and sat around the fire in temperatures below ten degrees. When Greening went to check on the herd, two caribou were lying down with the reindeer.

On this night, Mattie took the middle watch, from midnight to 4:00 a.m. He walked among the reindeer in the clear, cold night and was amazed at how he sank to his knees in the deep snow without his snowshoes while the deer walked over it. Noticing the two wild caribou milling about with the reindeer, Mattie saw an opportunity to stock up their dwindling supply of meat. He would talk to Cole in the morning about killing the two caribou.

Back at the campsite, the Sami family settled around a fire and camp of their own. Mattie took note of how close the family was. While they had been accepted by Cole and the others, they still kept to themselves.

Mattie could relate. Both his father and mother had died when he was very young and he was an only child. He had been passed around between several Mi'kmaq families, some of whom loved him and some who hated him. Mattie could never remember being a boy. He did recall one time, though, when he had tried to be one.

* * * * *

HE WAS STAYING WITH A MI'KMAQ family who had told him they were his cousins. They were camped a bit upstream from the mouth of the brook the white man called "Indian River." It poured into the northwest arm of Halls Bay, where he was told he was born. The Indian boy had heard many stories about the white man Hall who was captain of a schooner

The decapitated head of Hall, along with the heads of several of his crew, were found impaled on long, sharpened poles driven into the shoreline of the bay that would forever bear his name. The tale was told again and again by the white settlers as well as the Mi'kmaq Indians. With every telling it was said that the Beothuk Indians, who walked this land no more, had been responsible for the killings.

Curious to learn more about the cluster of homes built around the Halls Bay shoreline just north of the river, the young Mattie had walked until he was standing among the trees on the edge of the village his people called Wolf Cove. Several boys and one girl, all about his own age, were playing near the closest of the white houses. They appeared to be kicking around what looked like the bladder of an animal. Their screams of joy as they ran after the ball drew him out of the woods. Awhile later, he approached them.

The young girl saw him first. She let out a yell that hurt his ears and stopped the others in their tracks. They ran yelling and screaming in terror toward the house—all except one boy who was taller and who appeared to be older than the others. He had bright red hair that fell to his shoulders. Mattie had never seen red hair before.

Transfixed, he noticed too late the sharp-edged rock propelled from the redheaded boy's long arm. He turned to run back into the woods and the rock struck him a sharp blow just below his right kneecap, causing him to stumble. Looking back, he saw the redhead searching for another rock. At the same time, a white man with a long-barrelled gun gripped in his left hand rushed out of the house.

Mattie sprinted in fear and was soon lost in the trees. Feeling safe in the thick woods, he peered out. The young girl was standing and still screaming next to a woman who had a protective arm around her. The tall boy with the red hair was still throwing rocks into the woods. The man held the gun to his shoulder and pointed it skyward before pulling the trigger. He said something to the redheaded boy and then both of them walked back toward the woman and the girl. Before the sound of the shot had died, the young Indian boy vanished into the forest where no one followed and where he always felt safe. That was as close as the boy Mattie Mitchell had ever come to playing with anyone, Indian or white.

By the time he was ten years old he was trapping the streams and helping to provide for the family with whom he was living. They rarely went in any town, and when they did they stayed on the outskirts. They stayed apart from the whites. Usually he was hustled along with a small band of Indians on their hunting, fishing, and trapping excursions, during which they spent months on end by the banks of secluded rivers.

Standing there in the quiet, frosty night watching the deer and studying the heavens, he identified the North Star in the direction from which they had come with the reindeer. Not much had really changed, he thought. White children still avoided him and some of them still threw rocks at him.

* * * * *

MATTIE STAYED WITH THE HERD UNTIL the two dippers circling the North Star told him he had kept his watch. He walked back to the campsite, pulled a stick out of the fire, and pointing it toward the north. He laid it down in the snow, where it sizzled for a just a minute.

Crawling into the tent, he roused Greening, who went sleepy-eyed out into the cold. Mattie turned in, fully dressed. He hauled a dirty blanket over him and slept. When Greening ended his watch the two caribou had gone, and with them four of the reindeer.

They crossed dozens of frozen lakes and smaller ponds where the going was easier for Mattie. Now he would point in the direction he needed to go and the Sami would drive their charges ahead. The rest of the party would follow behind on the trail.

The party crossed hundreds of brooks, some of which they could jump across or step over on rocks. Other streams and rivers they had to wade across with warm boots removed and woollen trousers rolled up. Still, others they forded in waist-high water, necessitating quick fires afterward to dry out their wet, frozen clothing. At these crossings the sturdy reindeer shivered the cold water off their heavy coats, foraged whatever food was available, and looked around at the two-legged beasts standing and shivering by smoky fires as if curious what was taking them so long.

And always they were led by the tall Indian who seldom spoke.

Nine hard walking days later found the weary group of men, women, and dogs—none of the reindeer, not even the pregnant females, showed signs of fatigue—at Cat Arm. Once more Mitchell and Cole halted the trek. A sudden blizzard of snow borne on a northeast wind these first few days of the official spring date had made further travel unwise, but Cole wanted to keep moving. On the same day, all of the Laplanders suffered from snow blindness and they wanted to set up camp and stay there until they healed. Despite the severity of the weather, Cole had to "bally rag" them until they agreed to continue.

Everyone had run out of tobacco. They had to chop down spruce trees to allow the reindeer to eat the mosses that the Newfoundlanders called maw dow. Worse than that, they were down to the last of their flour and Cole had to ration everyone to one small doughy bread bun per day. They boiled water for the last of their tea, dried it, then boiled it again. The travellers were in desperate need of food. Killing one of the deer would be an absolute last resort.

On March 28, as they camped on a tributary of Sop's Arm Brook, Mattie fell victim from erysipelas again. However, when Cole asked him if was able to go get some food for the group, he agreed without hesitation. He and Greening left for Sop's Arm on March 29 with their two best dogs, Kruger and Black, pulling an empty komatik.

While the whiteout raged outside the flapping tents, Cole explained to the Sami, through the interpreter, that a storm this time of year was what the seal hunters called a lapping or whelping batch. It always came just in time for the birth of thousands of seals taking place on the immense floating icefields just offshore. When harp seals birthed or "whelped" their white-coated babies, they stained the virgin ice with countless spots of birth blood. The storm covered the creatures from predators while the newborns "lapped" their first liquid protein from the bellies of their lactating mothers. The storm of wind and snow always seemed to happen around this very date every year.

The spring date in Newfoundland, like spring everywhere else, was merely an easing-off of winter. There would be no fresh spring daisies to pick anywhere along their trail just yet, although the weather warmed on April 1 to an incredible thirty-five degrees with strong winds from the south. However, they learned it was only a "breeder" for worse days ahead.

Mattie and Greening had only taken one meal with them. They hoped to reach a small logging camp at the innermost reach of Sop's Arm that night. When they hadn't returned four days later, Hugh Cole grew very worried.

On April 4, 1908, he began to write in his personal journal:

> Rough weather continued all night. Thought the tent would have been blown down. By 8am tent nearly filled with snow. Snow coming through stove piping and door. Stove blown down. Marked trail from camp to brook in case the boys come that way. The weather too bad to face the brook. The brook is covered with huge snow drifts, but the boys will have a "trade wind" if they come back today. Another day gone and they have not arrived. Half a pound of meat left—enough for tomorrow.

> **APRIL 5TH**
> Still blowing, but not quite as hard. Snowing a little. Glass going up; temperature 22 above. Thick mist on the hills, no sign of the boys. Only a small piece of meat left—about 3

inches by 1/2 an inch. Told Sundine meat before sleep was not good for him. He looked so sad that I had to give way, and halve the beef, which I then cut into 13 small pieces. The tea was weak—and so were we. Gave instructions to Laps to move the camp on Monday towards Sop's Arm the direction in which the boys left. Will have to kill one of the deer tomorrow unless the boys arrive.

APRIL 6TH
Fine morning. Up early and cooked our little breakfast. Deer all collected by 6:30. Just about to pack up, when we heard a gun fired, on the hill about two miles away. We dropped our traps, and ran out of the tent. In the distance we could see Greening and five other men, with packs on their backs, coming towards our camp. Our two faithful dogs "Black" and "Kruger" were with them. Oh what joy. After a great welcome Greening said, "Where is Mitchell." Of course I looked at him with surprise, then he told me that Mitchell had left a day ahead of him with two men and provisions. Mitchell and the two men arrived in camp about two hours later. It appears that during the storm, they had crossed the brook at the steady, and wandered about 12 miles from the way.

(Mitchell and Greening left camp on the 29th ulto and did not reach Sop's Arm until the 31st. We reckoned the journey to be about 10 miles. It was not less than 30. These good fellows existed on one meal and were without shelter being compelled to leave the hills and take to the open brook. After travelling 15 miles, had to abandon the sleigh, as the dogs were too weak to haul. They were certainly "up against it," and it is difficult to imagine how they got through. They expected to find a mill at Sop's Arm; but, after searching until dark, they returned to a small salmon hut they had passed earlier in the evening. When they had made a fire, they "went to a cupboard," found an old tin can, which contained a little grease etc. Greening says it was awfully sweet. Sop's Arm was sighted in the morning about five miles from the huts. The few liviers there scarcely had sufficient food to meet their own needs. The nearest store was situated on the other side of White Bay and the ice had broken up during the week previous. This meant another spoke out of their wheel, as they thought of us in camp without food. The boys, who were now played out, sought for volunteers to make the trip across the bay, a distance of 10 miles. There was a great deal of slob ice in the bay, which made the trip a risky one; but the Sop's Arm men were ready in the morning. Whilst crossing, the wind changed, drove the slob in, and the boat became jammed. The going and coming took 52 hours, the men having to walk several miles on each side of the bay. Mitchell had collected some provisions and started off for camp before the men returned from White Bay. Greening and the five men were able to follow next day. Reference to my diary as to the state of the weather, will account for their slow progress. On Saturday and part of Friday travelling was impossible. The men carried no blankets with them—only packs and axes. Each pack weighing from 45-50 lbs.)

CHAPTER 15

BACK WITH THE EXPEDITION ONCE MORE, Mattie was relieved
to find them in good spirits. Maretta, the deaf and mute woman,
ran to greet him, stopped just short of touching him, and smiled
her welcome. The woman used a sign language that Mattie always
seemed to understand, and Maretta understood him.

The two men who had accompanied Mattie from White Bay
with the heavy load of provisions told Cole about their ordeal.
No "white man" could have ever done what Mattie had, they
said. The storm that had made them go astray had come on so
suddenly they were defenceless against it. Caught out on an open
barren with severe drifting and a biting wind, Mattie had led
them downwind to shelter. There were times, the men told Cole,
when they could barely make out the Indian's tall form through
the swirling snow.

What amazed the two men even more was, even when the
storm had cleared and Mattie realized he was well away from
where he wanted to be, he did not backtrack. He simply climbed
a rise, looked out over the hills for a minute, came back down,
and calmly walked in a different direction toward the campsite.
They believed the man had not in fact gone astray, but had just
been delayed because of the storm.

Their energy restored by the food, their spirit by the return of Mattie Mitchell, whom they all trusted to get them through, the band of nomads considered which way they would head from here. The men from White Bay returned to the coast. Cole, in consultation with his guide, had originally planned on trekking south to Birchy Narrows at the confluence of Sandy Lake and Birchy Lake, where they hoped to cross either of the two huge lakes on the ice and then on to Kitty's Brook.

Following the general course of Kitty's Brook would take them up over the barren lands of the Topsails and east across Sandy River—where Mattie had discovered the massive sulphide deposit in 1905—and then on to Millertown at the head of Red Indian Lake.

However, Mattie advised against this route. He pointed out that due to the mild yet high winds, the ice at the narrow ends of both lakes would almost certainly be broken up, if it wasn't already. The narrows between the two huge lakes always presented a danger while crossing because of the currents. Although the reindeer could easily swim across the lake anywhere, if the ice was unsafe the group of men and women would have to build rafts for themselves and their gear. Without the proper tools, this would be time-consuming.

The only other alternative, then, was to walk the entire length of the west side of Sandy Lake to the biggest lake of them all, Grand Lake. From there they would head west to the railway at Deer Lake. Mattie warned Hugh Cole that this route involved many river crossings that would be dangerous at this time of year. Cole agreed with Mattie's logic. He also had some concern about their limited food supply. Mattie mentioned quietly that there would be no communities to turn to for grub along this route. Again Cole agreed with Mattie's common sense. They would take an alternate route.

On April 7 the adventurers turned their backs on White Bay. With Mattie leading them on broken snowshoes, they wound their way up through the Long Range Mountains again and headed for Parson's Pond on the west side of the Great Northern Peninsula.

Mattie stopped to repair his snowshoes. The lashings were all but worn through in both shoes and the left shoe had a crack running diagonally along it for several inches. He used the last of his own caribou leather strips to tie a splint along the damaged shoe, as well as to repair the criss-crossed leather fillings. Cole and the others also took the time to repair their own snowshoes. All but the women, who only got out of the sleds on sharp inclines or dangerous places, had worn snowshoes daily and all were badly worn. The heavy snow still made travel impossible without the snowshoes. The day was late and Cole ordered everyone to see about their individual repairs. Mattie put his shoes back on and told Cole he would check out the way ahead. He left the others to set up a hasty camp.

This was an area Mattie knew well. He had travelled it many times, usually alone. He walked along the side of a steep rock formation that appeared ghost-like through the falling snow, hoping to find a way through for his group, and he smiled at the memory of this place.

* * * * *

HE HAD LED H.C. THOMPSON up this way from Bonne Bay in 1904. They had started their journey on a pleasant, warm summer day. Thompson wrote in his journal:

> We left Bonne Bay on August 29, and ascended to the high plateau that lies to the north of the bay by a landslide, or "scrape" to use the local expression, of over 1000 feet in

height, of exceedingly slippery blue slate, on which it was difficult to obtain a foothold.

Thompson marvelled at "his Indian's" astounding sense of direction and his knowledge of the country that was nothing short of "intimate." The two men traversed the Northern Peninsula for the next two autumn months.

They lived largely off the land. It was the "Indian summer" time. And every cool night, Thompson and Mattie sat by their fire, where Thompson compiled the first maps ever drafted of this majestic land. The geologist listened to Mitchell speak, only when asked, of the country they were walking through. He recorded bearings meticulously with his cherished compass, until, in this very place where Mattie now stood, with the cold night upon him, Thompson's compass had failed him! And he entered this, by the light of the cheery fire, into his journal:

> On September 4 we altered our course for Parson's Pond, not having to go on to the Sop's Arm Steady as we intended. The morning was misty, we hardly see twenty yards ahead of us, and the walking was difficult, the toil of forcing our way through the thick undergrowth being very great. We rose gradually to a broad, fairly even barren, with here and there a curious saddle-backed outcrop of granite generally from about 100-200 feet in length and 10 feet in width at the base, terminating at the top of a sharp ridge—a curious formation for which we were unable to account. There must evidently be much iron about, for the compass swung a good deal.

Mattie knew this place could be problematic for them, and not for the same reason that had confounded Thompson. Mattie couldn't use, nor did he need, a compass to get to Parson's Pond. Early on, just a few days into this journey, he had learned something about the reindeer that not even the Laplanders knew. The deer were afraid of heights.

The very first time they had followed Mattie to the edge of a steep incline, they had shied away. When he led them to approach it again, they had trembled in fright. Even when he took them down through precipitous cliffs, as had sometimes been necessary along their often treacherous route, the animals would roll their eyes up at the enclosing grey walls and remain skittish until they had passed through.

Mattie realized he would never get the animals down out of the high mountains here. Another way would have to be found down out of the hills to Parson's Pond. Thompson's journal:

On September 4 we took our way over a rocky, moss covered barren, fairly dry, and with comparatively little bog, and about mid-day we came to the end of the forge which lies at the back of the upper Parson's Pond. It is a deep-cleft ravine with cliffs nearly 2000 feet in height, rising almost sheer, and approaching to within a few hundred yards of each other. Between them winds a long sinuous lake which entirely fills up the gorge, and that the only way through it would be by making a raft. Beyond the lake we could see a low strip of green marshland, and beyond that the Azure sea. The atmosphere was of that extra-ordinary clearness which one so often finds in mountains after rain. The hills were cleft by ravines at short intervals, forming flat-topped barrens with abrupt sides, giving them, from the sea, the appearance of gigantic barns; that doubtless, as Archbishop Howley pointed out to me, being the origin of the French name "La Grange" of this mountain chain, of which the "Long Range" is probably a corruption. The sides of the gorge were too steep to be attempted with our heavy loads, and the timber, seen through our glasses, looked too small to make a raft with of sufficient strength to risk ourselves upon it on the lake, as the wind blows like a hurricane through these funnel shaped openings between the hills. There was nothing for it but to hark back along the crest of the Long Range to try and find an easier route.

And so Mattie "harked" his way back from the valley with the strange, iron-bearing rock formation. And with the "dark on his shoulder" and the snow finally stopping, he smelled the woodsmoke first and next the deer odour, and saw, through the trees, the flicker of a welcome fire.

Mattie had guided H.C. Thompson over a meandering route from Bonne Bay north as far as Flower's Cove. Their laborious hike had taken them out to the mouth of Sandy Bay River and along the "landwash" to Portland Creek. Then they went inland again as far as the big lake dotted with islands, which James Howley, the Newfoundland geologist, had named in Mitchell's honour in the late 1880s.

They had continued on their way mapping in the shortening days, inland from Daniel's Harbour, where Mattie built another raft to cross a long lake, with only four spikes that he forever kept in his pack to use again and again. He told Thompson that with these four rusty spikes he could "cross dis islan' all over."

And that night they slept beneath a blue mountain that Mattie called Naskwotchu. They walked back to the coast again to Port Saunders and along to Port au Choix, where they were graciously given passage across St. John Bay by a Captain Laurent in his own schooner, as far as Bartletts Harbour.

Mattie led Thompson inland again over the harsh terrain until they could see the blue waters of Hare Bay and the distant Atlantic on the northern end of the peninsula. West again to Flower's Cove, where the peninsula reached across the narrowing Gulf of St. Lawrence in a slight bulge for the coast of Labrador just a few miles away. Their journey just about done, they embarked aboard a steamer and sailed south to Bonne Bay.

Thompson carried in a waterproof bag all of the preliminary drawings, mappings, and intricate details of the land he had made by the yellow light of every night campfire. He had detailed the very first maps and sketched, complete with accurate compass bearings, this truly great Northern Peninsula. His work would be used extensively by explorers and adventurers of this land for generations after he and his intrepid guide had gone from the land.

From Bonne Bay, Mattie walked with Thompson to the railhead at Deer Lake on October 15, 1904, where the two men who had become friends bade farewell to one another. And Thompson said, after he had been complimented by his government employer, "The compass showed me direction, but Mattie Mitchell, sir, showed me the way."

* * * * *

FOR THE NEXT TWO DAYS, MATTIE searched for a way to lead the reindeer down out of the mountains to the coast at Parson's Pond. It was snowing again and the wind caused severe drifting. The going was difficult and very slow. They ran out of meat again. Cole ordered Mattie to take Greening with him and hunt for caribou.

The two men were passing the herd of reindeer, which had wandered off again—the deer always returned on their own now—when Mattie saw one with a lighter colour. It was a caribou! He killed the animal with one shot to the head using his Martin Henry rifle.

The closest reindeer twitched a bit at the sound of the shot, but the others merely turned their heads. The two men started to paunch the animal. When Mattie opened up its belly with his Bowie knife and the caribou's warm blood ran out and steamed onto the snow, the reindeer bolted, their hoofs clicking as they ran.

They hauled the entrails away from the hot carcass, cut the heart, liver, and kidneys away, cleaned the blood from the organs with snow, placed the viscera inside their packs, and fastened a rope around the head of the animal. With the two of them pulling eagerly, they returned to the campsite, with the caribou leaving a trail of blood growing ever fainter as they went. It had all taken less than an hour.

Mattie skinned the caribou whole and Greening cut the tender meat for the waiting pots. Mattie cut thin, green strips from the hide. He told Cole they would not last as long as cured leather, but they could be used for their snowshoe repairs. After filling their bellies with the freshly cooked caribou meat and a steaming cup of "switchel" tea—tea without sugar—Cole sent Mattie and Greening out again to find a way through the mountains.

To the traveller trying to find his way through treacherous wooded valleys, barren plateaus, and places where countless streams flow, a good vantage point is always a boon. A distant mountain, high ridge, or a distinctive lone hill, when viewed from one of these same landmarks, appears as if it could be easily followed. But when that same traveller comes down from the viewing point and stands beneath the smallest of trees before wending his way through a trackless wilderness, his landmarks have suddenly vanished and he is left with only his own sense of direction to guide him.

Mattie Mitchell was known for his incredible sense of direction. When he went the wrong way—a rare event—he would somehow know in just a few minutes that he had gone wrong and would immediately correct his way. To add to his problem on this day was the wind, which here on the flat-topped mountains seldom stopped blowing. It was snowing again, too.

He found a place where a man could get down a gorge by jumping on many tumbled boulders that had been dislodged by some long-ago erosion. The way also travelled beside a sheer drop-off, one the acrophobic reindeer would certainly not go near. And then, just as the light was leaving the land, he found a way to lead the deer down out of the mountains.

Now the two men made their way back to camp, not using the broken way they had come, but walking over new snow toward the welcome campsite and rest.

The snow had stopped some time during the night. The next morning dawned cold and clear. Twenty-two of the reindeer were missing and had not been seen since they had gotten the hot scent of blood from the slaughtered caribou. Cole had fed the dogs with some of the meat. They were running short of grub again.

Cole directed Mattie to lead him down through the pass he had found, to the settlement of Parson's Pond, where they would buy provisions and return with them to the herd. They made it after dark that evening as far as the abandoned oil wells by the saltwater pond itself, where they entered a deserted shack. They lit a fire in the small wood stove and slept soundly under a roof that did not flap in the wind.

Parson's Pond is a saltwater inlet that allows the North Atlantic waters inland almost to the foot of the mountains. Fresh water enters the pond from the streams on the hills nearby, mixing with the clear, salty ocean waters. In 1867, businessman John Silver was drilling for oil by the north shore of this brackish lake when he was stopped by the French government.

The French still claimed rights to this land, claiming the Treaty of Utrecht as their authority. This treaty, signed by the French nation in the city of Utrecht in the far-off Netherlands in 1713, ceded to the English all of their claims of eastern Canada, along with most of the coastal part of the island of Newfoundland. However, the French retained their age-old fishing rights to part of the island, according to article thirteen of that treaty:

> That part of the said Island, which stretched from the place called Cape Bonavista to the northern point of the said Island, and from thence turning down by the western side, reaches as far as the place called Pointe Riche.

It is worthy of noting that, in all of the negotiations that involved a land many times larger than both the French and English nations combined, the native peoples who inhabited the land were not mentioned. The English allowed the French fisherman exclusive rights to erect flakes for the purpose of drying the codfish and reluctantly agreed to temporary shelters limited to the fishing season. Silver's oil drilling did not fall under the fishing agreement, and the French, knowing they would never reap any benefit from oil along "their" fishing shores, protested. Amazingly, well over a century after the signing, the Treaty of Utrecht put a stop to Silver's enterprising venture.

Mattie Mitchell had witnessed that operation from a distance as an eager young trapper in his twenties. He had seen the same place drilled again in 1895, when the Newfoundland government discovered oil there. This venture too was plagued with problems, not the least of which was a financial one, and this latest operation failed, too.

Mattie Mitchell and Hugh Cole left the dilapidated shack in the morning without breakfasting and walked the five or so miles to the settlement of Parson's Pond. They arrived at 6:30 a.m. and were welcomed into one of the friendly homes, where they enjoyed a hearty breakfast they did not have to cook for themselves. After the meal they purchased supplies and headed back into the mountains with loaded packs.

And on April 15, Mattie Mitchell, in full stride and wearing torn snowshoes, came down out of the mountains leading the curious reindeer and the human troop behind him. Part of the way brought them to a very steep place and the deer snorted their obvious dislike, but the barking dogs and the yelling humans would not allow them to turn back. The stag that had been crippled by the dog was still lame and the rocky decline caused the animal much misery, so Cole ordered the reindeer loaded on one of the sleds, where it was tied securely and rode in style, like the Lapland women, down the south side of Parson's Pond.

Snow started again, and with the strong winds whistling in from the gulf bringing its Arctic chill to the land, Mattie led them through sheltered leads among stunted tuckamore. Here the reindeer found the food to their liking and the company had to drive them from the flora constantly. They swam the reindeer across St. Paul's inlet, where the animals seemed to enjoy the short swim and kept rubbing their bodies against the dories the humans were paddling, as if playfully hoping to dislodge their handlers into the water.

Just as dark came on the evening of April 8, Mattie's wife, Mary Anne, heard a commotion outside her door. Stepping outside she saw racing, barking dogs and yelling children, several men, and two younger women all hurrying along the snowy path that ran by her door into the hills. A distant barking from the green hills joined the village din and the echo of the excited dogs resounded around the quiet evening cove at Norris Point in Bonne Bay. Then Mary saw her tall husband come walking at the head of a bobbing bunch of animals, with the lowering shadow of darkness settling upon his broad shoulders. And that night Mattie slept under his roof and held in his arms the woman that he loved.

* * * * *

ALLOWING LITTLE TIME FOR REST, Cole got Mattie to take him to Deer Lake by a fresh dog team the next day. They arrived at the rail terminal at 6:30 a.m., in time to smell the fumes of the eastbound way-freight's struggling engine.

Mitchell returned alone to the herd in Bonne Bay the next day. The ice in the east arm of the bay was starting to break up and was unsafe for the reindeer to travel across, so Mattie led the group along an alternate route that he had walked thousands of times: around the northernmost end of the east arm to Deer Lake, where the reindeer browsed beneath the magnificent looming mountains on a land that Mattie himself owned. He led them down through the valleys and up over the mountain passes. They crossed the rising Lomond River at a steady, shallow spot that he knew of and headed southwest to Deer Lake. The lame stag was unable to walk, so they strapped it to a sled again and released it only at night to feed.

On April 24, the expedition arrived at the logging town of Deer Lake, where they were met by a well-rested Hugh Cole. Sundine, the Sami herder Aslic, and his wife and their daughter, Maretta, who stared in amazement at the first whistle-blowing locomotive she had ever seen, boarded the train at the railhead. Cole ordered four of the reindeer stags, two of which had suffered injuries on that last talus slope coming into Parson's Pond, and two which simply appeared to be "played out," loaded into one of the covered freight cars for the run east to Millertown. The other Lapland herder, Pere, Aslic's son, who had developed a friendship with Mattie, stayed with Mattie Mitchell and Greening to drive the herd to Millertown. All of the accumulated baggage from their trip south, including the komatiks and the dogs, were also loaded aboard the train. Cole left the three men one small dog and enough grub to last for two days before he departed with his entourage on the train, first class, for Millertown.

The trio set off on the last leg of their historic trek. The reindeer followed Mattie without encouragement. The lone dog trailed behind them silently with its tongue out. They travelled with relative ease along the railbed in the disappearing wake of the train. They left it where it crossed Kitty's Brook, well inland on the south side of Sandy Lake.

South and east for the next five days, Mattie led the party on the familiar way along the general course of the brook, which they crossed out of necessity several times as they went. Past the Gaff and Main and the Fore Mast in the distance, they walked and crossed south of the Mizzen Mast. Here, in the very heart of this island nation, the influence of the sea that surrounded it persisted. European explorers had given the rocky promontories that stood above this plateau the names of a fully-rigged sailing vessel, and by doing so the geological formations lost their age-old Indian ones. The four outcrops rose up out of the barren, windy landscape, like the permanently frozen pingos of the Arctic coast, and had always been used to guide the Indian people along their way.

This was a place Mattie knew well. He had hunted caribou here many times and had once led an American sportsman there to take a trophy stag with more than forty points. As he passed through the area, Mattie remembered the headless deer he had left on the barrens of the Topsails that day. The American refused to take any of the meat, and Mattie, who had to carry on his back the weighted, spreading antlers, was able to take only a few choice cuts from the carcass. He also remembered the Yankee sport taking the biggest, juiciest of the steaks out of the iron frying pan as soon as Mattie had cooked them by their campfire that night. He wished he had his pack filled with some of that meat now.

Down and away from the drifting Topsail barrens they made their difficult way to the thick, wooded valley where the Hinds

River rushed northwest toward the huge Grand Lake. He set rabbit snares every night in the alder beds and every morning he was rewarded with a brace and sometimes more of the tasty animals, which the three of them ate gratefully. Late one evening he crept up behind a beaver lodge. The big rodent was swimming back and forth in the small channel of water that opened beside its "pantry." He recognized it as a male and, knowing the female would care for the kits that were almost certainly inside the lodge, he killed the animal with one clean shot. That night the three men feasted on roasted beaver meat and, in the morning, with their bellies filled for the first time in days, they crossed the Buchans River and stood on the northern bank of the windy Red Indian Lake.

On April 30, Mattie strode into the Anglo-Newfoundland Development Company's camp on the banks of the Mary March River three miles northeast of Millertown. He and his group had walked 400 hard miles in twenty-six days and accomplished what many considered impossible to do in the dead of winter.

Behind him, with their flaring nostrils catching the scent of the four stags corralled nearby, the reindeer from Lapland waited until Mattie Mitchell stood aside, and then pranced the last few yards to the fence, where they poked their curious noses between the round, unpeeled pickets. Mattie had delivered to Millertown thirty-eight does and ten stags, all of them a bit leaner than when they had left St. Anthony.

Two of the animals had wandered off somewhere around the Parson's Pond area and enjoyed the local caribou's hospitality so much they never returned. It was reported that following autumn that a hunter from the area had in his sights a caribou that didn't look quite like any of the others he had killed. He killed it anyway.

Mattie Mitchell had carried out an incredible feat. He had led the expedition through what was, without doubt, the worst terrain in the country. He had achieved a feat as great as Daniel Boone, who had led another party through the Cumberland Gap of these same southern Appalachian mountains, only in Kentucky, forever changing the population of the great plains of America.

Unfortunately, the great reindeer drive was all in vain for the pulp and paper company. The deer didn't work out as suitable beasts of burden and were eventually sent back to Dr. Grenfell's Mission in St. Anthony. This time the reindeer didn't have to walk back over the peninsula but were shipped back in luxury — at no cost to the good doctor.

CHAPTER 16

MATTIE WAS NOW A *GISIGU* — AN OLD MAN.

One evening when he was returning home, his acute hearing detected a faint rustling sound coming from the alder beds near the gravel road ahead of him. He stopped and listened, but the evening had grown silent. A rabbit rustling through the falling autumn leaves, he figured, and he moved on. The sound came again and from the same place. Again he stopped and listened, but again no sound came. Curious now, he stepped forward. The noise repeated as before. Something was close to the ground and moved only when he did, as if hoping his walking would disguise its own movement. Mattie crept toward the brush where the sound had come from, leaned down, pulled some of the branches apart, and looked inside.

At first he saw nothing. Then the faint sound came again, very close, and at that instant he saw the owl. It was a little saw-whet no more then eight inches long. It was entangled among the thick alders, and when it saw Mattie it stood absolutely still and stared at him, its bright yellow-orange eyes with their huge black centres staring without blinking. The ground was covered with the hapless owl's feathers. Mattie could see it was injured but wondered why it hadn't just walked away. Then he saw the wire snare around its leg. The owl had been following along a rabbit lead and had become snared. With its frantic efforts to break the wire, it had damaged its wing against the tangled trees.

Pushing the trees aside to allow him room, Mattie bent down. With a soft crooning sound in his ancient language, he approached the bird, which now cowered close to the ground with its big, limpid eyes fixed on the Indian. He pulled the snare stick, which had been driven into the soil, free with one hand and held the shivering bird to the ground with the other. Mattie twisted the wire loose from the snare stick and reached to free it from the leg of the bird. He felt the blood-matted feathers. In its struggles to free itself, the owl had embedded the thin wire into its flesh all the way to the leg bone.

The bird was in terrible pain, but while Mattie gently removed the bloody wire, it made no sound and didn't move a feather. When the bird was free from its fetter it tried to stand, but fell back to the ground again. It looked up at Mattie pitifully. The owl could neither walk or fly. Mattie picked up the bird, which weighed a mere six or seven ounces, cradled it in the crook of his arm, and carried it home.

He coated the torn leg all around with the sticky myrrh from a fir tree. He pounded the thin inner white bark from a young aspen tree into a pulp and, stirring more of the spruce gum into the paste, he encased the wounded leg in the natural bandage. The fragile wing was more difficult to treat. Fortunately for the owl, the wing bone wasn't broken, only battered and severely bruised. More than half of the wing's long, white-tipped outer flight feathers were bent and useless.

Early the next morning, Mattie walked down to the landwash and brought back several small, greenish kelp bladders. He popped each one of them, saving the glistening drop of salt water they contained, then ground the kelp petals into a medicinal paste as he had done with the aspen bark. He smeared the medicine over as much of the bruised wing as he could. And while Mattie administered his gentle healing, the bird neither moved or uttered sound.

Hoping the bird would not flap the wing too much, he placed it inside a small, uncovered pen. The owl didn't try to fly out of the pen until many days later, when its wing had healed under Mattie's frequent doctoring. During that time Mattie caught meadow voles and mice and sometimes frogs for the bird, which ate whatever Mattie brought it.

Early one morning, when Mattie went outside, the bird was gone. Mattie was very pleased. His healing had worked. Then he looked up and saw, perched in a nearby tree, the owl staring down at him. He left his garden and went walking along the road. Hearing the flutter of wings behind him, he turned and saw the owl following him, flying from tree to tree and sometimes landing on rooftops and fences along the roadside. Its wingspan made it look much bigger in flight.

The bird soon became known as Mattie's owl—or that tall Indian's owl, depending on who you talked to. Everyone was amazed to see it follow him whenever he moved from his house, day or night. One of the Mi'kmaq words for owl is *gu'gu'gwes*. Mattie called the bird Gu'gu, but only among his own people. To others in the community he did not use the Mi'kmaq word for the bird, but called it "little nightbird."

The owl would follow no one else, not even when they tried to get it to do so. From the first morning when Mattie had seen the owl perched in the low branches of the tree, he had stopped bringing it food. But still, each morning when Mattie stepped from his door, Gu'gu was waiting in the same tree. When Mattie left the yard, the bird always followed.

The day came when Mattie was not able to rise from his bed.

He was dying and he knew it. Even his indomitable will was finally defeated by the state of near-death. From Marie Mitchell Sparkes's journal:

> My Grandfather had been ailing for a while, but on this particular day, he asked my father to go and bring him the priest so that he could receive the last rites of the church. And as he had been a devoutful Catholic, it was his last wish to have a priest present in his final hours. Back in those days the nearest priest lived in the Scared Heart parish in Curling which was a few miles south of Corner Brook. And since there were very few cars around the area, the more frequent type of travel then was by boat. So my father got in his Dory and rowed the few miles to Curling and returned with the priest, who administered the Last Rites to my grandfather.
>
> Later that night pop sat in the room by his father's bed with the holy candles lit and slowly flickering, sending their light around the room.
>
> My grandfather was awake and fully aware that it was his time to leave his earthly existence, he looked at my father and said "Johnny, I am going to sleep now" and with a sigh he closed his eyes for one final time.

And when Mattie Mitchell's body was carried from his home in the glorious autumn of 1921, Gu'gu, Mattie's "little nightbird," followed the slow procession as it made its way to the hill where Newfoundland's greatest frontiersman would forever rest. It was Indian summer, the time of year when hunters are mysteriously lured afield. And the Mitchell family laid their hunter down.

The gentle man who had contributed so much to the exploration and development of his beloved island home was buried on a hill in the west coast city of Corner Brook. Below him, the bay that he loved so much was calm and reverential in the still evening air. The mountain valleys were deep in shadow.

But the lofty mountaintops were tinged with the soft reds and purples that only come in the autumn time.

And as the cool night came down out of the hills, a new yellow moon appeared and, as it had on that long-ago night on the beach with the American adventurer, had the old one in its arms.

The mound of dark new earth looked even darker in the shadows. And from somewhere very near, a lone owl sounded its *skiew* of requiem and flew silently away before the day came, and never returned.

EPILOGUE

BRIAN SPARKES HAD AN UNEXPECTED and unexplained encounter with his great-grandfather, one that shocked and affected him for a long time afterward. Brian grew up listening to tales of his famous grandfather. Like his mother, Marie, he never tired of hearing them. She passed down most of these stories to him. He always secretly wished he could have met Mattie. He always wondered what he would say to him if given the chance. Brian never figured that one day he would tell his great-grandfather to leave and never return!

It was the autumn of 2005 and Brian Sparkes was forty years old. It was his favourite time of the year. The treed streets of the city of Corner Brook where he lived were resplendent with brilliant fall colours and the entire Humber Valley was dressed in autumn splendour. The days were short and the nights were cold and filled with glittering stars. Brian went to work as he always did. He was an appliance repairman and good at his work. It was just another day. But this night would be anything but ordinary.

When he went to bed that night, he was asleep as soon as his head touched the pillow. That was the strangest thing, and the only thing he remembered the next day. He remembered he hadn't been sleepy at all. He had decided he would read for a while, though he wasn't much of a reader. Brian was reaching for a book when he suddenly changed his mind and turned out his reading light. He had no memory of falling asleep. That time between consciousness and slumber wasn't there. He had no idea how he knew, but he *did* know he was dreaming. Even in his dreaming state he knew he was dreaming.

He was staring down at the tall body of Mattie Mitchell, who was in a coffin of clear glass. His great-grandfather's face looked just like the photos his family had of him. His clothing did not. Mattie was wearing a grey uniform with stripes. Brian could not figure out the style. It didn't look like the uniform of a soldier. Mattie had never been a soldier. He wore no hat. His long hair was as black as a rainy night sky. On his feet he wore the long, leather, laced-up leggings evident in some of his pictures. The boots nearly came up to his knees. The coffin's lid was closed, but Mattie's eyes were not.

No matter how Brian turned, the eyes of his great-grandfather followed him. For several minutes Brian stood above the glass coffin, unable to escape the stare of the corpse that lay within.

Without closing his eyes or speaking one word, Mattie, with the glass coffin, suddenly floated out of sight, down a magnificent green river that flowed through a valley of golden colours. Brian cried and cried for his great-grandfather to come back. But the glass coffin, glistening with light, disappeared around a bend in the river. The valley turned green, the water turned black, and Brian awakened bathed in sweat and tears.

Brian told no one about his dream. The images he had seen in the night were so powerful they stayed with him all day.

Then it happened again. That night was a repeat performance of the night before. It was exact in every detail: Mattie in his glass coffin, his wide-open eyes, the green river, the golden valley—Brian crying like a child for his grandfather to return. This happened for several more nights.

The strangest thing of all was that Brian did not want to dream about Mattie after the first night. He wanted the dreams to go away. Yet in his dreams he always cried for Mattie to return when the glass coffin sailed down the green river.

Brian was afraid of the nights. He hated the thought of going to bed. He even tried staying away from his room as long as he could, hoping a late hour would give him a much-needed dreamless sleep. Nothing helped. The dreams kept coming, but still he told no one.

He was driving home one evening and for some reason had driven a different way. He was passing the cemetery road when an idea came to him. He would visit his great-grandfather's gravesite and ask him to stay away from his nights. Walking along the grassy pathway to the place where Mattie Mitchell rested, he wondered what he was doing here. After all, who had such weird, recurring dreams, and who in his right mind would come to where the dead lay, with such a strange request?

The evening was late. The sun was down below the hills, and everything was quiet and still. When Brian reached Mattie's gravestone, he bent down and noticed the fresh flowers his mother had placed there. Brian looked all around to see if anyone was near. He wondered if he should talk to Mattie aloud or simply think his thoughts.

He decided to speak aloud. When he began to talk to his great-grandfather, a wonderful peace stole over him and he didn't feel strange at all. He suddenly realized he was crying. For some reason it felt just fine to talk to the old hunter. Brian simply asked Mattie—he didn't say great-grandfather—to please stay out of his dreams.

"I am proud to be a part of your bloodline. I love you, Mattie."

Still sobbing, Brian straightened up from the grave and turned away. Just before he reached his car, he heard a sound behind him. Brian was sure it was the cry of an owl. He looked back and thought he saw a small shadow flit over Mattie's grave. He waited for a few more minutes, but he neither heard or saw anything more.

That night, Brian Sparkes slept in peace. The next day, he remembered the date. The day he had asked his great-grandfather to stay out of his dreams had been the eighty-fourth anniversary of Mattie Mitchell's death.

And the image of Brian's great-grandfather came to him no more.

AUTHOR'S NOTE

DURING THE COURSE OF MY RESEARCH to write what I soon discovered to be the incredible story of Mattie Mitchell, I read extensively from many works written by the early European explorers. Many of them recorded their investigations in great detail. Some of them were great authors and wrote with a wonderful flowing hand.

Considering the attention they paid to some details, the omissions I found in many of their writings bewildered me.

Leaving the port of St. John's and usually travelling at government expense, they always named the ship they sailed on, its captain, and sometimes even some of the crew members. After arriving at one of the major outports like Twillingate, for example, they would record the schooner names and their skippers who took them farther into the bays.

Often they required smaller vessels to take them to the mouths of rivers or deeper into the dangerous bays as needed. And again, they almost always named the men who carried them forth. But, when taken by the Mi'kmaq Indians up the unknown rivers and deep into the mysterious wilderness beyond the white man's frontier, they simply referred to them as their "Micmac Indians" or "my native guide" or "my Indian." The Mi'kmaq guides, who led them to shorelines that few white men knew about, remained nameless.

There are, of course, a few pleasant exceptions, such as James Howley and Alexander Murray, who were undoubtedly Newfoundland's greatest non-Indian explorers. I acknowledge, as well, Hugh Cole for his vivid, daily accounts of the 400-mile-long reindeer trek. To these men I give full credit.

Throughout my research I found that the contributions made by the Mi'kmaq people to the exploration of insular Newfoundland are exemplary. They were called upon extensively as guides. And by far the one who was requested most frequently was Mattie Mitchell.

In 1891 he played a major role in leading the Reid surveyors to the right areas to allow access for the first Newfoundland railway. He guided them along the west coast as well as much of the central part of the route.

Mattie led the first mapping expedition of the Northern Peninsula, the first major geological survey of practically all of central and western Newfoundland.

He guided European explorers through the hidden valleys and over the top of the Annieopsquotch Mountains, which admirably lives up to its name in the Mi'kmaq language, meaning "Terrible Rocks."

It should also be noted that Mattie took his son Lawrence with him on many of his excursions. The American sportsman-clergyman Worcester recorded fourteen-year-old Lawrence with his father on at least two occasions. In 1904 the A.N.D. Company hired Mattie and Lawrence to find timber and other resources, however, Lawrence is not recorded as part of the group that discovered the Buchans ore body in 1905.

Alfred Charles William Harmsworth, 1st Viscount Northcliffe, born just outside of Dublin, Ireland, would have no other guide than Mattie Mitchell. Harmsworth especially loved fly fishing for Atlantic salmon. He was a newspaper publishing magnate in England, who added the pulp and paper mill in Grand Falls to his list of assets in 1905. In that same year he was added to the British peerage as Baron Northcliffe.

Mattie Mitchell was also recognized by the British royalty. After guiding members of the royal family on a very successful hunting and fishing expedition, he was verbally given the sole rights to hunt and fish the King George IV Lake area in central Newfoundland forever. Although Mattie never exercised this right, it would have been interesting to see what would have happened if that royal "decree" had been put in writing.

There is another, much more serious event recorded in the private memoirs of Marie Sparkes. It involves Mattie's discovery of the ore body on Sandy River. She records that Mattie was receiving a guiding fee of $18 per month at the time. The barrel of flour he received as a bonus, valued in 1905 at $2.50, has been universally scoffed at. It has also been considered by others as fair. After all, Mattie was in the company's employ, for which he was getting paid. When he was asked what he would like for his discovery, Mattie promptly said, "A barrel of flour fer me family's winter bread."

But Marie has carefully recorded a much more sinister account.

A.N.D. Company officials came to her grandfather's door while he was away from home for an extended period. The officials wanted a paper signed and, in the absence of Mattie Mitchell, obtained a signature from a visiting relative of the man. The relative of Mattie didn't have a chance—or was probably unable—to read the document that he signed. Sadly, the family have not been able to find any evidence of such a document. It was the belief of Marie Sparkes that it would prove little more than the signed agreement of the Mitchell family to forgo forever any benefits from their grandfather's historic find.

Elwood Worcester, the American sportsman who came to Newfoundland to experience caribou and black bear hunting, as well as salmon and trout fishing unequalled anywhere, spent many years on the island with Mattie Mitchell. The man kept coming back for more than the hunting and the fishing. He came for the experience of living in a wilderness with a man who, when he walked away from the confines of the smallest of habitations, was truly a part of the natural whole. Worcester recorded and left behind a detailed description of his time spent with Mattie Mitchell. I acknowledge his contribution to my effort.

I have gathered much of the information in this book from the handwritten lines of a remarkable woman, Marie Mitchell Sparkes. After my second reading, I sensed between the fluid lines of her work a hidden personal yearning to have her grandfather's life known. Hers was a quiet voice that hoped to be heard, and her steadfast resolve was quieted only by her death, which came far too soon.

Within the pages of Marie's beautifully written work I found a woman with a desperate need to have her history revealed. I also witnessed the early days of a child whose history was cruelly denied. Along Mattie Mitchell's "paths to pages" I have felt the burning need in Marie Sparkes to shout her ancestry.

I have merely whispered it.

There is within me a great fear that I have failed, after reading the personal feelings of a woman who clearly longed for the exploits of her grandfather to be heard by everyone.

Marie's dedication to making her remarkable ancestry known has thankfully been handed down to another equally enthusiastic advocate of the Mi'kmaq culture. To her son, Brian Sparkes, I am forever grateful. Brian entrusted to me—which I reluctantly accepted—a satchel filled with rare photos, memorabilia, and documents written by his mother, Marie, about Mattie Mitchell. Until then, no one outside of their immediate family had seen them. Like his mother, Brian never met Mattie Mitchell. Brian grew up in an entirely different era than did his great-grandfather, and even a different one than his mother. However, their Mi'kmaq ancestry has finally been accepted.

It has been a slow road.

* * * * *

In 1998, the government of Newfoundland and Labrador recognized Mattie Mitchell's contribution to the growth and prosperity of the province by opening the Mattie Mitchell Prospectors Resource Room, under the Department of Natural Resources. The facility is located in the department's Geological Survey on Elizabeth Avenue, St. John's. Its mission statement on the provincial government's website says it "is designed to support prospectors by providing them with mentoring, technical support, and promotional assistance, thereby assisting in the creation of wealth and jobs through sustainable mineral development."

In 2001, the Historic Sites and Monuments Board of Canada recognized Mattie Mitchell as a person of national historic significance. A renowned Mi'kmaq hunter, guide, and prospector, Mattie Mitchell contributed to the exploration and mapping of the Northern Peninsula, and to the development of the new Newfoundland economy and mining of the twentieth century.

In 2005, a plaque in Mattie Mitchell's honour was placed at the Deer Arm site on the main highway within Gros Morne National Park.

ACKNOWLEDGEMENTS

I would like to thank the following people for their respective contributions to the creation of this book: Brian Sparkes; Ray Nielson; Valda Bowe-McGuire; Gerald C. Squires; Sean Rumboldt; David McDonald; Tony Huxter; Faron Knott; Allan Keats; and Peter Oram.

To my wonderful friend and wife, Rose: you are my confidence.

I respectfully acknowledge Garry Cranford for his idea of having me write about Mattie Mitchell. His dedication to the constant recording of Newfoundland and Labrador history is to be commended. I hope I have exceeded his expectation.

To Margo Cranford, whom, with my very first book, stood by my side and assured me I was deserving, and whom has kept my guard through many public appearances, the sincerest of thank yous.

I also recognize the effort made by my editor, Jerry Cranford, in the production of this book. For a non-outdoors city boy to edit the life of Newfoundland's greatest frontiersman could not have been easy for him. Thanks, Jerry.

BIBLIOGRAPHY

Anger, Dorothy. *Noywa'mkisk (Where the Sand Blows . . .): Vignettes of Bay St. George Micmacs.* Port au Port East, NL: Bay St. George Regional Indian Band Council, 1988.

Assiniwi, Bernard. *The Beothuk Saga.* Toronto: McClelland & Stewart, 2001.

Barnes, Michael. *More Than Free Gold: Mineral Exploration in Canada Since WWII.* Renfrew, ON: General Store Publishing House, 2008.

Coish, Calvin. *Stories of the Mi'kmaq.* Grand Falls, NL: College of the North Atlantic, 2000.

Encyclopedia of Newfoundland and Labrador. 5 vols. St. John's: Newfoundland Book Publishers, 1981–84; St. John's: Harry Cuff Publications, 1991–94.

Higgins, Jenny. "Pre-Contact Mi'kmaq Land Use." Newfoundland and Labrador Heritage. http://www.heritage.nf.ca/aboriginal/mikmaq_land_use.html.

Jackson, Doug. *On the Country: The Micmac of Newfoundland.* St. John's: Harry Cuff Publications, 1993.

Johnson, Arthur, ed. *Hugh Cole's Reindeer Trek down the Northern Peninsula of Newfoundland: 1908, March 4 to April 30.* St. John's, 1962.

MacLeod, Pat. *Gros Morne: A Living Landscape.* St. John's: Breakwater Books, 1988.

Marshall, Ingeborg C. L., ed. *Reports and Letters by George Christopher Pulling Relating to the Beothuk Indians of Newfoundland.* St. John's: Breakwater Books, 1989.

Martin, Wendy. *Once Upon a Mine: Story of Pre-Confederation Mines on the Island of Newfoundland.* Montreal: Canadian Institute of Mining and Metallurgy, 1983.

Murray, Alexander, and James P. Howley, *Geological Survey of Newfoundland.* London: Edward Standford, 1881.

———. *Geological Survey of Newfoundland Reports, 1881–1909.* St. John's: Robinson and Company Limited Press, 1918.

Penney, Arthur E. *Nestled between the Hills: A History of Cannings Cove.* St. John's: Jesperson Press, 1991.

Peters, H. R. *The History of Mining in Newfoundland, 1857–1949.* N.p., n.d.

Speck, Frank G. *Beothuk and Micmac*. Vol. 22, *Indian Notes and Monographs*, edited by F. W. Hodge. New York: Museum of the American Indian, Heye Foundation, 1922.

Tompkins, Edward. *Ktaqmkukewaq Mi'kmaq: Wlqatmuti / The Mi'kmaw People of Newfoundland: A Celebration*. Corner Brook, NL: Federation of Newfoundland Indians, 2004.

Whitby, Barbara. *The Last of the Beothuk: A Canadian Tragedy*. Canmore, AB: Altitude Publishing Canada, 2005.

Whitehead, Ruth Holmes. *The Old Man Told Us: Excerpts from Mi'kmaw History, 1500–1950*. Halifax: Nimbus, 1991.

Above: Marie Marion Mitchell Sparkes, granddaughter of Mattie Mitchell, Corner Brook, 1998. (Courtesy of Brian Sparkes)

Below: A handwritten excerpt from Marie Sparkes's personal papers. (Photo by Clint Collins)

> Many years have passed since I first started my journey of delving into the past to uncover the many great and astonishing feats of my Grand Father and as one year turned into another I was able to learn more and more about his adventures and his great Contributions to the island that he loved.

Matthew "Mattie" Mitchell and Alfred Charles William Harmsworth, 1st Viscount Northcliffe. (Courtesy of Brian Sparkes)

GARY COLLINS

Above and below: Sean Rumboldt holding Mattie Mitchell's prayer book. He is a direct descendant of Mattie's and lives in Lewisporte, Newfoundland. (Author photo)

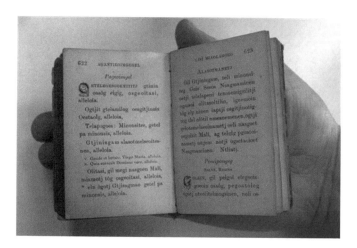

Above: Santu and her son, Joe Toney, in Gloucester, Massachu-setts. It is believed that they are descended from the Beothuk. Below: Joe Toney. (Photos from *Beothuk and Micmac* by Frank G. Speck)

Lapland herder Pere Sombie, age thirty, and reindeer. Unidentified man beneath reindeer is believed to be in the process of milking it. (Courtesy of Tony Huxter)

Matthew "Mattie" Mitchell (left) and two sportsmen.
(Courtesy of Brian Sparkes)

GARY COLLINS was born in a small, two-storey house by the sea in the town of Hare Bay, Bonavista North. He finished school at Brown Memorial High in the same town. He spent forty years in the logging and sawmilling business with his father, Theophilus, and son Clint. Gary was once Newfoundland's youngest fisheries guardian. He managed log drives down spring rivers for years, spent seven seasons driving tractor-trailers over ice roads and the Beaufort Sea of Canada's Western Arctic, and has been involved in the crab, lobster, and cod commercial fisheries.

His writing career began when he was asked to write eulogies for deceased friends and family. He spent a full summer employed as a prospector before he wrote *Soulis Joe's Lost Mine*; he liked the work so much, he went back to school to earn his prospecting certificate. A critically acclaimed author, he has written a total of six books, including *Cabot Island*, *The Last Farewell*, *Soulis Joe's Lost Mine*, *Where Eagles Lie Fallen*, and the children's illustrated book *What Colour is the Ocean?*, which he co-wrote with his granddaughter, Maggie Rose Parsons. The latter won an Atlantic Book Award: The Lillian Shepherd Memorial Award for Excellence in Illustration.

Gary Collins is Newfoundland and Labrador's favourite storyteller, and today he is known all over the province as "The Story Man." His favourite pastimes are reading and writing, and playing guitar at his log cabin. He lives in Hare Bay, Newfoundland, with his wife, the former Rose Gill. They have three children and three grandchildren.

Gary Collins can be reached by email at **nicholasc68@live.ca**.
The official Gary Collins website is **www.garycollins.ca**.